D0368046

The Last Kiss

A true story of love, joy and loss

Leslie Brody

The Last Kiss

A true story of love, joy and loss

Leslie Brody

Title Town
PUBLISHING

The Last Kiss

A true story of love, joy and loss

TitleTown Publishing, LLC
P.O. Box 12093 Green Bay, WI 54307-12093
920.737.8051 | titletownpublishing.com

Editor: Amanda Bindel
Front cover photo and design: Susie McKeown, susiemckeownphotography.com
Back cover and interior layout and design: Erika L. Block
Author photo: David Adornato

PUBLISHER'S CATALOGING-IN-PUBLICATION DATA:

Brody, Leslie, 1961-

The last kiss : a true story of love, joy and loss / Leslie Brody. -- 1st ed. --
Green Bay, WI : TitleTown Publishing, 2012.

p. ; cm.
ISBN: 978-0-9852478-6-7

Summary: Six years after their wedding, Elliot was diagnosed
with pancreatic cancer. Told with heart, humor and compelling
immediacy, this is a love story about a passionate marriage, the
importance of loyal friends, and the resilience of children coping
with the illness and death of a father.--Publisher.

1. Pinsley, Elliot Alan, 1951-2008--Death. 2. Cancer--Patients--
United States--Biography. 3. Terminally ill--Family relationships.
4. Spouses--Death. 5. Children of cancer patients--Psychological
aspects. 6. Bereavement--Psychological aspects. I. Title.

RC265.6.P5 B76 2012
362.19699/40092--dc23   1210

Printed in the USA
first edition ♺ printed on recycled paper
10 9 8 7 6 5 4 3 2 1

CONTENTS

to Elliot
and Alex, Devon, Max, Kate and Aaron
with love and gratitude

Elliot in Captiva, Winter 2008

PROLOGUE

"That place where you are is the best place I've ever been."
—Letter from Elliot

I never bought a video camera when my kids were little for fear it would be a curse. It was my one and only superstition. As a newspaper reporter I had met too many anguished couples who peered desperately into home movies of their children as if sheer desire could make their lost babies spring back to life. Those heartbroken parents gave me the vague premonition that if I started shooting videos myself, a day would come when I would pore over them in grief.

Then I decided I was being silly and we were missing out on all the giggly oohs and aahs of revisiting our holidays on the screen. A house like mine and Elliot's, with five kids from two first marriages, could be complicated. I thought filming our good times together would give us proof that we had finally become a family.

My first impulse turned out to be right. I was just wrong about who would be taken from me. Almost as soon as I started making home movies, we learned my husband was going to die. There was an inoperable tumor in his pancreas, an organ I couldn't even locate. Doctors said if we were lucky, Elliot would live for a year or two.

Of course I can't blame the damn camera. The timing simply turned out to be one of those cruel ironies: At the height of our happiest days, we were forced to learn how to live in the face of unbearable loss.

That quiet grey video camera quickly became my ally, my tool for saving tender little scraps of the life I wished I could save for real. Still photos would never do justice to Elliot, whose face is—was—constantly in motion, expressive, animated with warmth and love and humor. His dark brown eyes were infinitely deep.

I saved all his emails too. Fortunately he ignored my cautious warnings not to send personal messages from his desk at *Bloomberg News*.

"HEY YOU," he wrote me a few months before he died, when pain searing down one thigh signaled the cancer was spreading. "I just want you to know I'm thoroughly consumed with amorous thoughts."

Determined to remember as many details as possible, I saved love notes, my endless to-do lists, the kids' handmade get-well cards and instructions for administering antibiotics through a home IV. That sheet has crinkled spots from drops of saline. Another page has ink blurred by tears. I also scribbled down funny moments that made me smile, hoarding them like a squirrel that would depend on them later for sustenance.

"Honey, I'm on the way to the store," I said over my shoulder one day as I hunted for my car keys. "Do you need anything besides methadone?"

Elliot burst out laughing. It sounded like I was just running out to pick up some milk, not heavy duty painkillers. There were months when living with terminal illness began to feel almost routine.

More often, though, it was wildly emotional—when we raced to the emergency room yet again or kissed one last time before nurses wheeled Elliot off on a gurney through thick operating room doors for yet another risky procedure—and I wondered, ashamed, if my days felt richer and more fascinating because of all this drama. When this ordeal was over, would normal life seem flat? Like when Dorothy comes home at the end of *The Wizard of Oz* and the movie switches from color to black and white?

Maybe, but I had bigger things to worry about. I had to memorize our marriage.

The camera captured the ordinary moments: Elliot relaxing on the couch to watch a Mets game, ranting about something outrageous in *The New York Times*, or regaling the kids with tales of a gigantic food fight back when he was a troublemaker at Hebrew school ("Matzoh balls were flying!"). I was careful not to train the lens solely on Elliot for long. I didn't want him to know I was engaged in such a morbid project as recording his life for a future without him.

But documenting what matters is what we did for a living—we'd even met in a newsroom—and I wanted to keep him with me this way. There was no real hope he'd get better. Two specialists at the top of their field gave him the same prognosis and a quick check of statistics showed why. Only six percent of pancreatic cancer patients lived five years. Most didn't last nine months. The best chance for survival was catching the disease early enough for surgery. In Elliot's case, it was too late.

So we didn't waste precious time shopping for another doctor who would say what we wanted to hear, or scouring the Internet for a cure, or buying into the quack who argued for an enema made out of coffee. Elliot hunkered down to endure whatever his doctor advised so he could stay with us as long as he could. And I tried to figure out how to do my best for the first man I truly loved, the first to truly love me.

Here was the knife. I didn't know how to deal with my conviction that by leaning on each other through this unwanted odyssey we would get to know each other even better, and come to love each other even more, and then his death would be even harder to bear. Should I protect myself by backing away?

"I finally found the right man and now I'm going to lose him," I cried on a social worker's couch about a week after Elliot's diagnosis. I'd gone there in search of a guide to keep me from collapsing. "How am I supposed to take care of him knowing we're going to get ripped apart?"

"Don't be afraid to get closer," she said. "The people who recover best after a loss are often the ones with the strongest bonds. The people who have a harder time are usually the ones with conflicts or regrets."

"But we've been married only six years," I went on. My children had finally grown close to Elliot. All our kids had adjusted. "How am I supposed to stay positive when I know this is going to end badly?"

"Don't focus on staying positive," she said, handing me yet another tissue. "Focus on staying in the present. He's here now. You really don't know what's going to happen. Nobody knows what will happen to any of us."

I am so grateful for that advice. "Don't be afraid to get closer" became my mantra, one I'd repeat to myself when we were teetering on the edge of the abyss. We held on to each other tight, with a desperate determination, and that made us stronger still. We were braver together than either of us could be alone. Even now, I believe with all my heart that the depth of our connection has given me the strength to survive his loss.

Now I find I like to watch our home movies and wish I'd taken lots more. In most scenes you can't even tell Elliot was sick. He never lost his hair, light brown with lots of gray.

Here he is at the beach in Cape May, playing catch on the sand with the boys. He jumps to grab a ball out of the air.

"Did you get that one?" he shouts to me. "That was my best catch!"

Here he is a year later at the ocean in the Outer Banks, laughing as he runs out of the water to escape a monster wave. He's thinner now, and if you know where to look you can see the bump of the port implanted under his skin near his collarbone where an IV tube attached for chemotherapy. He looks lean and fit, handsome and exuberant because all our kids are out there splashing.

And here he is showing off a dinner table he's set for two in our backyard on a summer night. The kids are away, and to surprise me he balanced dozens of tiny votive candles in the crevices of our rock wall. They flicker like diamonds in the dark. "Welcome," he says with a mischievous grin, "to my little love grotto."

Some people say they don't want to remember a man when he was sick—they want to think back on the better days. But those two years and four months of trying to stave off the inevitable were, in truth, a beautiful time. We focused on living, not dying, and I don't want to forget a minute of it. Writing this book is my way of keeping those days safe, protected from the fickle distortions of a fragile memory. I yearn to have my husband back, I long for his jokes and his passion and his body, but I am at least grateful that we didn't squander the gift we had for loving each other.

"He's here now," I kept telling myself.

Leslie and Elliot

TWO WEDDINGS

In my experience, the quality of the wedding bears little relation to the quality of the marriage. My first was all tuxedos, white tulips and elegance but didn't work out in the end. My second was slapdash but gave me the world.

Elliot Alan Pinsley (changed from Pinsky by a relative after Ellis Island) was my second husband, and to some people—especially my parents—he seemed like Mr. Wrong. They had been much more gung ho about my first husband, Emile Camille Geyelin III, whose affluent upbringing matched my own.

When I first said "I do" I was twenty-eight, unsophisticated about love and sex and what it took to be a real partner. Growing up at Brearley, a prestigious all-girl prep school, I had never experienced boys as real people. I had a big sister but no brothers. Men seemed foreign, something glamorous to catch. My mother's only romantic advice was simple: "If you talk about him all night, he'll have a wonderful time." That worked for getting a second date but proved a great way to end up with a narcissist, too. I had a string of dashing short-term boyfriends (in my twenties I even went on a date with Warren Beatty but didn't kiss him because he was almost twice my age). My favorite beau was a Portuguese fencer who greeted me after a match by lunging to tap his epee against my cheek. I almost swooned. These guys had looks, charm and accomplishments, but they didn't care a whit about me.

I met my first husband when we were both reporters in the hopping Tampa bureau of *The St. Petersburg Times*. He was athletic and wiry with fine-boned features, and I was drawn to his simmering, mysterious intensity. Known by the nickname Milo, he was an intrepid investigative newshound, a fierce mix of intellect and self-reliance. His elite background was impressive too. His father, once the head of *The Washington Post*'s editorial page, won a Pulitzer Prize for his essays against the Vietnam War. Milo's mother, descended from the family of Civil War General William Tecumseh Sherman, was a fixture in Washington society, constantly entertaining diplomats, journalists and political luminaries. Once *Vogue* ran a photo spread chronicling how she whipped up a fancy dinner for twelve on twenty-four hours' notice.

When Milo got a plum job at *The Wall Street Journal* in Philadelphia, we dated long-distance for months. Then I grew weary of plane trips back and forth.

"We should settle down or break up," I announced one day. Milo gave in.

And so I did the thoroughly un-modern thing and quit my great job to get married. It was a puzzling move for someone who had been so determined to get the best grades in school, to get into the Ivy League, to get one hot assignment after another. I was always looking ahead, pushing toward the next step—mostly because deep down I was shy and driven to rack up a resume to prove that I was worth loving.

Back then it was a source of pride that in seven years, I'd had five jobs and eleven apartments in two hemispheres. After Yale I'd flown off to Japan to teach English and ended up at The Associated Press in Tokyo, covering earthquakes, jet crashes and trade disputes. Using my overtime pay to zip around from Bali and Bangkok to Burma, I felt like quite the jet-setter. When I was ready to come home, I got a job at *Fortune Magazine* in New York, but really wanted to work at *Time*. I asked an editor there what it would take to get hired.

"Go to a newspaper and show me you can write," he said.

And so I'd landed in Florida. But my glowing resume papered over the truth that all my moving around had left me lonely. College friends were getting married and I felt left behind, like there was a race to check off that milestone too.

My wedding to Milo was gorgeous. It was in my parents' elegant townhouse off Park Avenue, a home so stylish it was once featured in *Elle Décor* magazine. With contemporary art on stark white walls, black wood floors, tall ceilings and minimalist modern furniture, it was as airy and pristine as an art gallery. A burglar broke in once and when the cops came they gasped. They thought the thief wiped the whole place out. Actually, my dad told them, it's always like this. The intruder found nothing to take.

The townhouse had plenty of space for 150 guests in black tie. The second floor living room where we exchanged vows on a Saturday night in January 1990 was lined with extravagant quince flowers and long tapered candles. It was decorated by an A-list florist, a man mentioned with reverence in the pages of *New York Magazine*. The pheasant pie came from a caterer whose clients included Jacqueline Onassis. There was a jazz band for dancing on the third floor, a classical string duo during dinner on the fourth and a magician for Milo's young nieces and nephew on the fifth. All under eight years old, they were dolled up in forest green velvet dresses and shorts, custom-made by my mother's tailor.

I felt oddly detached as the night flew by in a festive blur of champagne and congratulatory air kisses. My mother, the editor of a niche art publication, was a perfectionist about parties, and she set the whole thing up. I didn't get too involved. Maybe that was a bad sign. The only thing I chose was my dress, a long white Mary McFadden with narrow crinkly pleats like the gown of a Greek goddess.

Milo and I bought a house high on a hill in Montclair, New Jersey, about twelve miles west of New York City. It was simple but had a magnificent view of the Manhattan skyline. (The view from the dining table and my bedroom window has kept me sane for almost two decades. The glorious sunrises, the hypnotic clouds and the pink reflections of sunsets on skyscrapers always make me stop and look. Even on my most hectic days, its sheer beauty brings me back to the broader, lasting world outside my antsy head.)

Milo was a good man, the kind I thought I was supposed to marry, but what we shared—camaraderie, privileged upbringings and aspirations in journalism—was not enough to sustain us. As the years went by, what I once respected as independence I began to resent as withdrawal, especially when I was struggling to take care of two young children and working part-time at *The Record*, a suburban New Jersey daily. I craved support and affection, and the gap between us grew deeper. That was my fault too. Always averse to conflict, I didn't express what I needed. In time it became impossible to keep going in a relationship that lacked warmth, connection and desire. As Lynn Redgrave once said, "Loneliness within a marriage can drive you mad."

When Milo and I agreed to separate seven years after our beautiful wedding, it was done with great civility. In contrast to our flawed marriage, we had a model divorce. A few times we even found ourselves laughing together over a funny turn of phrase at the mediator's office. My one gnawing fear was the pain we were causing our children. But it can't be good, I told myself over and over, to grow up with unhappy parents. Our daughter, Devon, was four when Milo moved out. Our son, Alex, was one. The months surrounding Milo's departure passed in a wrenching haze of guilt and anxiety and desperate hope that the kids would be okay. We did our best to separate with kindness. Still, it was heartbreaking to watch Alex, so little, sob with hurt confusion when we first started the every other weekend and Wednesday night handoffs, his quilted diaper bag passing back and forth between the grownups, along with our stiff smiles.

The second time around, my groom had none of the pedigree or detachment of my first husband. Elliot was the son of a printer in Queens. He grew up on malted milk shakes offered as bribes to go to Hebrew school and relished his summer job as a fourteen-year-old delivering fabric for a garment dealer. His boss gave him cab fare to keep the goods clean, but Elliot would take the subway and spend the cash he saved on meatball heroes.

Ironically, these two very different men, coming from such disparate origins, ended up on similar paths. Both fled the Northeast to go to the University of Wisconsin in Madison. Both found their calling at the college paper, *The Daily Cardinal*, just a few years apart. And both ended up covering legal news for bastions of New York financial journalism.

While Milo grew up surrounded by power, Elliot was raised on romance. His father printed the posters for Broadway shows and used to take Elliot to musicals like *South Pacific* and *Carousel*. Elliot adored all those songs about soul mates and passion and the healing power of true love. He grew up hoping that some enchanted evening, he would see a stranger across a crowded room.

That crowded room turned out to be the messy, grey-carpeted fourth-floor of *The Record* in Hackensack. It would be years before we acted on our attraction, but once we did, we felt inseparable.

My second wedding was almost nothing like my first, and that was a good thing. This time I took charge. I wasn't going to ask my mother to organize a ceremony she didn't support. She was concerned about all this upheaval for her grandchildren, and that I could understand. I was worried too.

To keep the day as relaxed as possible, I booked a Sunday lunch in June for two dozen people at Arthur's Landing in Weehawken, a restaurant with a spectacular view of Manhattan across the Hudson. My parents and a few city friends could come by ferry. No designated drivers necessary.

The challenge was finding someone who could marry us there. We didn't want anything religious. After several leads proved fruitless, I picked up the phone book. Lo and behold, in the yellow pages under "weddings" was a guy who promised to deliver whatever ritual you wanted.

There was no time to wait until Elliot could come with me to check him out. On my next weekday off, I drove an hour to the man's house somewhere in Central Jersey with my little boy in tow. Alex was about to turn four, all blond hair and freckles and mischief. I brought toy trucks and pretzels and a sippy cup of juice to keep him busy.

When we arrived at the wedding guy's slightly unkempt ranch house, two couples in shorts and t-shirts were perched on his living room couches, thumbing awkwardly through fat binders with the prices for various services. The wedding guy—I don't remember his name—wore a golf shirt that showed his beer gut spilling over his belt. Maybe he was a truck driver who got licensed to run ceremonies through the Internet. The whole scene was a turnoff, but I didn't have much time to look further.

"Please just don't say anything about God," I told him. "Nothing spiritual or New Age-y either. We want to keep this simple."

He charged two hundred dollars.

A few days before the big day, my father called.

"I'd like to pay for your wedding," he said, direct as always. I told him that wasn't necessary, he had already given me a big one, but he insisted. I was deeply touched. Like my mother, he had reservations about this marriage but his determination to pay for it told me he was doing his best to get on board. Maybe he recognized that it would be almost impossible for me to find a man he thought was good enough and that I was serious in my choice. Perhaps he also saw that I was following a bit in his footsteps. When he married my mother, their parents were appalled. My mother's family in the South couldn't believe she picked a Yankee, no less a Jew. Despite such censure, my parents had been together for more than four decades and were still devoted to each other.

Elliot and I got married on June 24, the day before I turned thirty-nine. It was a scorcher. The air was thick and hazy with humidity. When we woke up at my house—we broke tradition and spent the night together before our nuptials—there was a note slipped under the bedroom door. It was from Devon. She had written it in royal blue crayon on white construction paper in slanted capital letters.

DEAR MOM AND ELLOT,

HAVE A HAPPY WEDYN! ELLOT IS A GRAT STEPFOTHR! AND MOM IS A GRAT MOM! AND KATE IS A GRAT STEP SISTR! AND MAX AND AREN ARE GRAT STEP BURUTHRS!

LOVE DEVON

My heart filled with gratitude for such an enthusiastic endorsement. Elliot kissed me and went off to thank the author. I took a deep breath and tried to inhale confidence. It was a moment of calm before the onslaught. The house shook with feet pounding up and down the stairs as Elliot's kids and mine took hurried turns in the shower. Elliot put on the new brown suit he bought for the occasion and looked quite dapper. I'd found a silvery grey sleeveless top and long teal skirt in matching silk with narrow crinkly pleats. The material, which resembled that of my first wedding dress, was the only reminder of my first time around. Somehow the Greek goddess theme stuck with me. Elliot's mother, always kind, gave me the pearl necklace that Elliot's late father had given her long ago.

We made it to the restaurant just before our relatives and friends. The wedding guy came in a dark suit at noon and was clearly in a rush to get going. He had another gig to officiate.

As our guests chatted over flutes of champagne in our private room with floor-to-ceiling views of the Empire State building, I snuck into the ladies room for a moment alone. It was cool from the air conditioner, but that didn't stop my nervous sweat. Crescent-shaped stains were creeping out under the arms of my silk top. My stomach was in a painful knot. It was hard to smile through a ceremony that my mother disapproved of. I just wanted to get through it so Elliot and I could escape to the beach in Bermuda. I took a deep breath, steeled myself and walked back out into fray.

Elliot's children, Max, a shy twelve-year-old, and Kate, quiet at sixteen, sat by a window looking subdued. Aaron, nineteen and home from college, was gregarious as always. Devon, in a classic pink dress with a satin bow and white patent leather Mary Janes, was excited about being the flower girl. I gave her a basket of rose petals to toss. When she realized the room had no aisle to parade down, she pouted in disappointment but perked up when my sister's little girls arrived. I had brought along new boxes of crayons and Lego kits for making bulldozers in case they needed extra entertainment. Alex, wearing a white button down shirt and navy blue shorts with suspenders, ripped open his box before the service even started.

Soft jazz piped in from the main dining room.

"If someone doesn't turn that down," the wedding guy barked, "I'm going to get a gun!"

Could he be any tackier?

As soon as Elliot and I brought our children together in the center of the room, the guy started. It was impossible to focus on his words about devotion and trust and tolerance. As Elliot's fingers entwined with mine, I kept looking at the kids to see if they were okay. Kate touched a knuckle to the corner of one eye. It's hard not to cry when you see concrete evidence that the family you grew up with is gone for good, or at least dramatically altered. Max pinched the top of his nose with his fingers but would later swear he wasn't tearing up, really, just tipsy from his first sip of champagne.

"You are, ALL OF YOU, part of this new family that Elliot and Leslie have committed themselves to," the guy said to the small crowd of guests standing around us. "It is a great and wonderful challenge they have taken on. There will be days it may seem daunting. They will need every one of you."

I stole a glance at my mother. She was sitting in back, outside the circle, looking the other way, far into the distance. She was trying in vain to choke back tears. So was I. Any marriage is a gamble, and it feels like an even bigger risk when you're bringing children along who could suffer from any bad bets. I was scared. Maybe this would turn out to be a huge mistake. Maybe I was being selfish. But it had taken me half a lifetime to find a man I loved who loved me so much, just the way I was, and I couldn't bear to give him up. I didn't want a life ruled by cowardice.

"Leslie and Elliot, this day not only solemnizes your marriage," the guy continued, "it also honors and celebrates the family you have formed with Aaron, Kate, Max, Devon and Alex. Young members of the family, please join Leslie and Elliot and all hold hands in a circle."

Alex, who had wandered off to work on his Lego bulldozer, heard his name called and came over to stand next to me. He looked a bit stunned to be in the spotlight.

"Family is not about a blood relationship. It is a construct of the heart. You are now, and for all time, married and a family."

Devon's eyes grew glassy. She sniffled. Aaron squeezed her shoulder and she looked up at him. He gave her a grin and she smiled back.

That was a gift, just what I needed to see. The kids were so sweet, and so sweet to each other. They're adjusting, I told myself. It's the grownups who are having trouble. I think we're all going to be alright. This is going to work. I have to make it work. We have to. We'll fly off on our honeymoon, wash our worries away in the ocean and come back to start life fresh.

My father came over to shake Elliot's hand and kiss me on the cheek.

"Just be happy," my dad whispered in my ear.

Elliot reporting for *The Record* in Haiti, 1986.
Photo courtesy of *The Record*.

THE THINGS HE CARRIED

Elliot always schlepped a knapsack—to work, to baseball games, on vacation. When the blue one he adopted as a hand-me-down from his youngest son wore out I got him a simple black one from L.L. Bean. It always had a book, an umbrella, computer screen wipes that he used to clean his glasses, Band-Aids, pens, and, after he got sick, condoms. To his horror, doctors said that we had to use protection when he started the highest octane drugs—otherwise the most intimate acts might dose me with his chemotherapy. He hated the feel of those slippery things, but he put up with them for my sake and had to confess it gave him a youthful little kick to fumble with the wrapper like a lusty teenager. Ever optimistic, he always carried a few Trojans in his knapsack's front pocket so he'd be ready for anything, anywhere. I just hoped my kids never unzipped that pocket to hunt for a Lifesaver.

Aside from our amorous adventures, one of Elliot's favorite times of the week was Saturday morning. He believed in long, languorous breakfasts eating pancakes, reading *The Times* and railing against finger-in-the-wind politicians, corruption on Wall Street and ridiculously overpaid athletes with bimbos on their arms. He savored hashing over the previous day's Mets games, initiating my son into the manly world of sports stats, criticism and fierce loyalty to the team he'd rooted for since he was twelve, saving milk carton coupons for tickets to Shea Stadium. He'd cheer for those scrappy underdogs no matter how much they disappointed him year after year. He told Alex that being a Mets fan built character.

"What a bunch of bums," Elliot would grumble, shaking his head in exasperation. "My eighty-year-old mother could throw better than that."

"Yeah," Alex would nod soberly. "Mine too."

Some people thought of Elliot as a bit of a kvetch, but they just didn't get him. Most of his gripes struck me as comedy shtick, just venting to get aggravations out of his system. He'd carry on about Montclair mommies who blocked the road to chat in their minivans, breakdowns on NJ Transit and those rolling briefcases that took up the whole damn sidewalk. He was sincerely irritated by such offenses but knew his condemnations were excessive. They were largely meant to entertain, and he always made me laugh.

When it came to serious injustice, his complaints stemmed from real outrage. His anger was the flip side of his passion. As a determined young reporter, he wrote heartbreaking accounts of the custody trial of Baby M, whose surrogate mother changed her mind about giving up the little girl she had promised to another couple. He wrote about mistreated war veterans and Haitian children so poor they bathed in sewers. At the office, his criticisms of bad editing decisions and favoritism felt to me like a tender form of sharing. He talked to me more openly than any man ever had.

My parents never got him. They saw complaining as a character flaw, a sense of victimhood. To make matters worse, sometimes Elliot looked down to the side while he was talking so he could concentrate without distraction. My father found that terribly rude.

"Why can't the guy look me in the eye?" he asked me once after they met. I didn't have a good answer but knew Elliot was unaware of the transgression. And he always looked straight at me.

It sounds embarrassingly superficial and backwardly un-feminist, but Elliot's hair was the first thing that caught my attention. When I first saw him in *The Record*'s newsroom back when I was thirty-one, before my first child was even conceived, his desk was near mine. Every afternoon at 3:00, after fixing a grilled cheese sandwich at home for his little boy, Max, he'd rush in for a night rewrite shift and dump his worn leather briefcase on his desk.

Elliot didn't seem to notice me, but I'd sneak peeks at his hair. It was light brown, straight, shiny and thick with a side part. Sometimes the front sweep of it would fall forward over his forehead as he read, and he had a seductive way of tucking the side strands behind his ear. When he was deep in thought he would slowly stroke the narrow beard that lined his jaw. It looked vaguely French. I don't generally like beards and moustaches, but his looked dashing, even necessary, to frame his long face. They set off his deep-set eyes, high cheekbones and easy smile. He always joked about his big nose. To me it looked virile.

"Hi Elliot," a blond reporter who sat next to him said every afternoon in her teasing *can-you-believe-we're-back-here-again?* voice.

"Hello Laurie," he always echoed back, low and gravelly. He never said hi to me—and I was too timid to say anything to him—though years later he would swear that his first thought when he saw me walk through the newsroom was "What lucky guy is married to her?"

Elliot didn't want to be at *The Record* again. He'd already had a nine-year stint there four years earlier and was tired of toiling away at a mid-sized daily that dwelled mostly on the meat-and-potatoes of New Jersey suburbs. When he first joined the paper he'd covered some big stories, like the blow-up at The Three Mile Island nuclear plant. He'd won a reputation for his can-do attitude, fairness and elegant writing style. Although he had once dreamed of becoming a foreign correspondent for *The New York Times* in Paris or the Middle East, his ambition ebbed when his first baby, Aaron, was born. Completely besotted, Elliot maneuvered for a cushy position as a feature writer that let him get home for dinner and bath time. Elliot would get right in the tub with his splashing son. When a group of fellow reporters made a run for *The Los Angeles Times*, he moved too slowly. By the time he applied, *The Times'* hiring spree was over, and he wasn't such a great self-promoter anyway.

After he had a daughter, Kate, and another son, Max, Elliot's skill covering federal courts earned him a job at *Manhattan Lawyer* magazine. He loved the rush of working in the city, but as soon as he was promoted to be a columnist, the magazine folded. With a young family to feed, Elliot needed a paycheck fast, so he swallowed his pride, clenched his jaw and headed back to *The Record* in much less glamorous Hackensack. Lucky me.

I got to know Elliot well in 1994, about two years after my start there. He had become an editor and was assigned to help with a long-term project investigating the state's child protection agency, the Division of Youth and Family Services. I was one of three reporters involved and found myself looking forward to getting back to the office to tell Elliot what I had seen in a case file or learned in an interview. He was so engaged, so sympathetic to the children in these ravaged families, and so interested in what I had to say. I had just had my first baby, and he got a kick out of my gushy tales about Devon's first teeth and her refusal to nap unless a specific cube-shaped pillow was wedged against the very top of her head.

That DYFS project was almost a catastrophe, a career killer, thanks to one reporter on the team. Call him Scruffy. He claimed to have dramatic evidence that DYFS workers knew a little girl was in danger at home but left her there anyway; the parents ended up beating her to death. Three days before his stories were supposed to be published in a big Sunday splash—the first of our series—Scruffy admitted sheepishly that he needed to tone down some of his strongest conclusions. As Elliot grilled him over the course of an editing session that lasted until almost midnight Thursday, Scruffy confessed he had stretched the facts a bit here and there. As he squirmed and stepped out for serial smoking breaks, the truth became clear. He had jazzed things up to win a prize.

The rest of us were furious and panicked. Radio ads had already promoted Scruffy's bold exposé. At least my stories, detailing the impact of addiction on the families in the system, were ready as a fallback. They weren't nearly as sexy, but they were accurate. It was an obvious substitution, and editors told me to come in early Friday for last-minute fact-checking.

I worked hard and fast all day while the newsroom tom-toms beat wildly about the mess. Reporters who had long mistrusted Scruffy were thrilled he'd finally been caught.

In the late afternoon, though, I was puzzled to see all the top editors and layout people crowded into one small glass-walled office. Their faces looked solemn. Elliot was in there too, his arms folded tensely across his chest. I caught his eye and crooked my index finger at him to come out.

"Don't tell me they're still dithering about whether to use his stories," I said.

"They're trying to see if anything in them can be salvaged."

"But that doesn't make any sense. Can you please tell them I want to talk to them?"

There was barely room for me to stand.

"We saw a reporter self-destruct here last night," I told them, trembling. "Those stories have no credibility anymore. I can't be part of a project or a paper that prints them."

I wasn't bluffing. If those stories were printed, it would have been easy for the state to lay bare his bogus claims. Our professional reputations would have been ruined. Our mistake from the start was giving Scruffy the benefit of the doubt when he went off reporting on his own. He was a blowhard with a street-smart swagger, and we got conned. Elliot had told a supervisor about some misgivings early on, but they were dismissed. Scruffy was the top editor's pet. Until that Friday.

Finally the editors committed to killing Scruffy's installment and swapping in mine. One thankful editor told me privately—and I agree—

that they would have done the right thing eventually, but my ultimatum saved them precious time.

Elliot and I went to my computer for a final comb-through of my stories.

We sat down in two swivel chairs next to each other, knee to knee, looking at the same screen. The first thing Elliot did was tap out a message.

"I am so proud to be working with you," he wrote.

I smiled, so proud to have him say so.

He offered to drive me home that night—my car was in the shop for some reason—but I said no. In the heart-pounding intensity of the moment, and the deep relief of a crisis averted, I was afraid I might kiss him.

Years went by. I had a breathtaking baby boy and savored time with my kids on a long maternity leave. But there were serious problems at home. My marriage was on the rocks. So was Elliot's.

Elliot and I used to have lunch a lot in the office cafeteria or a diner, and that continued after I got back from my leave. He had always had close women friends and as much as I liked him it seemed to me I was one of the crowd. Then one day he suggested a nicer destination than usual for lunch, an Italian place with white tablecloths and low lighting, and he ordered a vodka, then another, and then he took a deep breath and told me he wanted more than a friendship. I had been feeling much the same way but would never have dared to say so. I thought I'd always be admiring him from a certain distance. I don't know how I replied to his admission. I was scared and thrilled and reluctant. I had a baby and a preschooler and a broken marriage to officially untangle through the long, arduous process of divorce. I was afraid to do anything that might throw dynamite on the path. But Elliot was so handsome and funny and caring and there was something magical about our attraction. At the end of that lunch he walked me across the parking lot to open my car door and he kissed me, a real kiss, deep and hungry and searching.

I had never felt so wanted. But it was too soon. I got in my old green station wagon and slammed the door and drove off in a daze. I almost had an accident. He called the next day to take a walk in a park.

"It's a glorious day," he said. "And we let a pretty big genie out of the bottle. We can't just stuff him back in."

And so it began, with slow steps toward a kind of happiness I never dreamed I'd be lucky enough to find.

Courtship when you have children is a tricky thing. After some time had passed and I felt ready to have the kids get to know Elliot, food became a crucial ingredient in their introduction. One day he surprised us by knocking on our door early in the morning with a brown paper bag full of bagels. Back then he was living in a cheap apartment in Bloomfield while his separation got hammered into a divorce. He began to make a habit out of showing up for breakfast sometimes before speeding up the Garden State Parkway to pick up Max for school.

"It's the bagel man again," my daughter Devon would say when she spotted Elliot through the window as he walked up our front steps.

"That's nice," I'd reply, tickled and nervous as I opened the door to the clean fresh smell of his shaving cream. I wondered what my kids were making of all this. They seemed amused, curious and glad for the special treats. Sometimes he brought chocolate chip muffins. Alex, who couldn't pronounce Elliot's name, called him Oggie, as if it rhymed with "doggie." We even painted a mug with the nickname so Elliot could have something of his own for coffee when he came over. We spelled it O-g-g-i, like the Italian word for "today." In the present was where I wanted to be. The recent past with my first husband was so thorny and the future was so uncertain.

One day Elliot brought each of my kids a set of huge red plastic costume lips that covered their own. They sat in their pajamas at breakfast with these fat red grins like demented clowns. It was just so goofy. They loved it, and I loved seeing them have so much fun with this man so full of enthusiasm. He brought so much life into our house.

If Elliot couldn't stop by, there would often be a bagel waiting on my desk when I got to work. Or a chocolate chip cookie. Or a foul ball snagged at a baseball game. Elliot got to his editing desk at 8:30 a.m., before almost anyone else, and thought nobody knew the source of these little gifts. Of course there were no such secrets. Reporters are professional gossips. It's probably delusional for anyone in any office romance to think nobody knows.

It wasn't wise but he flirted by email. "Your shoulders look lovely today" he typed as soon as I took off my jacket on a hot morning and hung it on my chair. "How am I supposed to concentrate?"

Feeling my cheeks flush I threw my jacket right back over my sleeveless top, covering the shoulders he had nuzzled just a few nights before. I was afraid he'd be fired for indiscreet behavior or abusing the company computer and kept telling him to stop, but he was recklessly romantic and ignored all my warnings. As much as I protested those notes, I ate them up. They made coming to work so exciting. His effusive messages were filled with comforting comments about articles I'd written, funny anecdotes about his kids and descriptions of places he wanted to take me, the ballet or a concert or a restaurant in New York. It was a relief when he got recruited to edit legal news at *Bloomberg News* in Manhattan. That put some professional distance between us.

After we'd been seeing each other for a while Elliot brought his children over. I'd met them before when they visited the office but it was different under these circumstances. Through the window I watched Kate, with her long blond hair falling forward to shield her face, and Max, his shoulders hunched, shuffling up our front steps in single file, looking serious and unsure.

"Hi," I said with a smile when I opened the door.

"Hi," they said back. The air was stiff with awkward silence but we gritted our teeth and plastered on our smiles until we got to a dark movie theater where nobody had to talk. Getting to know them couldn't be rushed.

Elliot was in a hurry to get married, even have a baby. I wasn't. I'd messed up a marriage before, was afraid I'd screw up again and thought the kids needed more time to get to know him. But he was impatient and determined. He hated feeling like an island, no longer head of the home where his kids lived in Hackensack and not officially part of mine in Montclair. At times we fought about our future. Slow down, I begged.

But how could I resist a man so sweet he snuck into my house to vacuum and mop while I was on a ski trip with my children? A man who filled the house with pink and white roses to apologize for pushing me too fast? How many men are so quick to say they're sorry?

"Hi," Elliot wrote in a note to welcome me home. "If you notice nothing else, be sure and check the freezer. Bottom shelf. I'm sure you could use a treat. It's your favorite. Nuts aplenty."

It was homemade butter pecan ice cream from Holsten's, a local soda fountain that would one day be world famous as the set for the very last scene in *The Sopranos*.

"There's also apple juice, milk, chicken nuggets and some other stuff so you don't have to rush out to the store first thing….I hope you'll accept my handiwork as a symbolic deposit to my vastly overdrawn account at the forgiveness bank…I hope you realize how hard I'm working still to win your love, your heart, to help you out in every way I'm able so you can be happy and strong and confident that beyond this difficult time, you and I will make a great pair. All that will be left is an amazing, life-giving love. You'll see."

As I got to know Elliot's kids I tried to be warm but not overbearing. To their great credit they were friendly back. On weekends we took whoever was willing on hikes or bowling or to baseball games. Devon saw Kate as the ultimate in cool with her layered tank tops, grownup books and edgy tastes in music. Alex worshiped Aaron, who was big and burly. To my distress and Alex's pure delight, Aaron gave him wild piggyback rides and picked him up by his head. Sometimes they all clashed with Max, the introspective one in the very middle. Max thought I babied my kids too much. Probably so. But there's one thing I did get right. I always had good food around. Everyone feels more at home in a casual kitchen. We had barbeques and brownies ad infinitum. Still, it would take many months for us to feel truly comfortable together. It would take years to feel like a family.

ITALY
June 2006

Elliot was a good driver, but those steep, narrow, winding roads along the rocky Italian Riviera were frightening. Some snaked between high stone walls and came to T-intersections at angles so sharp you could see the cars careening towards you only when they flashed into dusty round mirrors hung at the corners.

This trip marked our sixth wedding anniversary. Elliot said it was my present for putting up with all his "mishegas," his favorite Yiddish word for crazy behavior and being an all-around handful. As wonderful as it was that he wanted to whisk me off on romantic escapades, those herky-jerky car rides to ancient ruins and seaside restaurants made my whole body tense, my hands poised to push away the dashboard if we crashed. We had rented a big clunky Volvo—all the zippy mini cars had stick shifts that I couldn't handle—and sometimes it felt like sheer momentum would send us veering off a cliff.

Things seemed safer in the Tuscan countryside, the roads more predictable. Our simple hotel in Siena sat right outside the Roman gate. Our room one flight up had only what it needed, an inviting bed covered in a fluffy white quilt, an antique wooden dresser with sticky drawers and a magnificent view of the rolling fields.

"This must be the world's most beautiful bathroom window," Elliot announced with a satisfied sigh.

Standing at the sink you could see the breakfast patio below with its clay pots of bright pink geraniums and tables with white linens set for two. Chirpy birds pecked at bread crumbs and fallen prosciutto. Looking farther into the distance, you could see misty fields and cypress trees in countless shades of green.

"We could just spend the rest of our vacation in here," he said with a smile. "Then you wouldn't have to get in the car."

It sounded like fun to have lunch at a working vineyard, so we made reservations for the next day at the Verrazzano estate about an hour away. It had belonged to the family of the sixteenth century explorer who navigated New York Harbor. The very name suggested adventure.

We set off in the morning, running late as usual due to one of Elliot's luxurious soap-up-twice showers. We arrived just in time for a tour of the tangled grape vines, the giant oak barrels, and rows upon rows of bottles of red wine growing better with age. All delicious, you'll see, the guide said with practiced charm, but don't wait too long to drink it or it will turn to acid.

His sales pitch grew more heated over lunch as tourists got tipsy and compliant at long wooden tables laden with local olives, heaping platters of roast pork and glasses of increasingly extravagant Chianti. Two couples sitting next to us were Persian doctors who had escaped Iran right before the 1979 revolution. They made for cosmopolitan company, a reminder of just how wide, open and colorful the world could be, so far from the narrow groove of deadlines, commutes, carpools and chores that threatened to consume us at home. Elliot was always an ardent defender of our sacred date night every Wednesday, and we savored our time alone on weekends when the kids were busy, but this was a whole new freedom, our longest getaway yet.

Elliot was relaxed as he talked, laughed and squeezed my knee under my blue silk skirt. How handsome he is, I thought. How lucky we are. How great it will be to get back to our cushy white bed.

The climax of the meal came when we tried the vineyard's own balsamic vinegar. The guide said to chew a little piece of parmesan cheese and keep it in on your tongue. Then sip a drop of vinegar from a spoon. Mix it in your mouth. It tasted divinely rich, salty and tangy sweet like tamarind. They actually called it "love potion." We wanted to bring some home.

At the counter Elliot fumbled. He seemed dazed from wine and a touch of indigestion. That was the very first hint of what was to come.

"You got the most expensive kind," I blurted when I looked in the paper bag. It was fifty-six euros, or about eighty-two dollars then, for a tiny square bottle. "The big twelve euro version would be fine."

"That's okay," he said lightly. "We deserve it."

Elliot drove home slowly, taking in the late-day sun, his hand on my thigh, my hand on the back of his neck.

"I love you so much," he said. "I love that we can take this trip."

"I love you too. Thank you for all of this. It means so much to me that you put it all together."

A little while later, he winced. He shifted in his seat, loosened his belt with one hand and readjusted his jeans. He couldn't get comfortable. He pulled into a gas station to find a bathroom and disappeared for a disquietingly long time. It was too bad, I thought, that he didn't wait until we got back to our hotel bathroom with the fabulous view.

The problem was too much rich food, we figured, but the sharp twinges in his abdomen didn't go away. The next morning at breakfast, when Elliot asked the grandmotherly waitress for plain toast and rubbed his stomach with a sad grimace to signal he needed some medicine, she fluttered around with consternation.

"Chamomile tea," she insisted. "Make you better."

BE A GLADIATOR
July 2006

Elliot still felt odd pains when we got home. Easy fixes didn't work, so he went to a gastroenterologist. Elliot hinted darkly that maybe it was cancer—his father and several uncles and aunts had died of it—but I thought he was being melodramatic. A suspicious swelling on a CT scan suggested he might be right, but then an MRI seemed to rule that out. The specialist ordered some other tests to be sure. It would take a few days for the results to come back.

I was sitting at my messy desk one Thursday afternoon, deep in an assignment on the frenzied debate over early admissions policies at elite colleges, when my phone rang. It was Elliot, calling from the *Bloomberg News*room.

"There's a tumor," he said.

The concept of cancer didn't sink in for me. Tumors can be benign, after all. His doctors still didn't know the exact origin of the thing, so the possibility of something dire seemed too foggy, mysterious and unreal to take seriously.

"The doctor said you can call him if you have any questions," Elliot added.

That caught my attention. Doctors don't often volunteer for a sidebar with a patient's wife. The receptionist got the doctor on the phone for me right away. I still didn't utter the C-word. Neither did he.

"Elliot's very upset," I said. "Is he justified?"

"He's justified in being upset but not despondent," the doctor answered, similarly vague.

That was pretty much the entire conversation. My twenty-plus years as a reporter asking pointed questions evaporated right into the ether. I just didn't want to know.

Elliot was sent for an endoscopy—a tiny camera on a tube pushed way down his throat—to confirm the suspected diagnosis. The test didn't show any clear masses, but the GI guy referred us to an oncologist anyway while scheduling another type of endoscopy. It felt like we were on a sinister and perplexing treasure hunt, with no good reward at the end.

"What's the matter with Elliot?" my kids kept asking.

"We're not exactly sure," I said. "The doctors are trying to figure it out."

I found myself dressing a little sexier, cooking fancier I-love-you dinners as a distraction. I made grilled lamb chops with mushrooms sautéed in garlic and trout with ginger sauce, even though he wasn't eating much and was barely drinking wine. He'd lost twelve pounds in six weeks and was looking even more alluring and fit than he had in years. Like most middle-aged men, he had wanted to drop a few.

On the first Sunday in August, we took one of our precious trips for two to Lambertville, a cheery village of cobblestones, bistros and antique shops on the Delaware River. It was a stunning sunny day and we sat outside to have crab cakes and Caesar salad. It felt wistfully sentimental. I couldn't help wondering if this would be our last semi-carefree romantic lunch. Hell might break loose at the oncologist's office the next day. I tried to savor my last moments of ignorance.

As always, we went to the Phoenix, a used bookstore. I hid in the back leafing through a book called *50 Essential Things to Do When the Doctor Says It's Cancer*. I didn't want Elliot to see that, like him, I was giving in to the idea that this dreaded disease might really be the issue.

"The cancer journey can be a time of joyous discovery of inner strength and the beauty of life," it said.

Yeah, right, we'll see. We already knew we had a wonderful thing going and appreciated every minute of it. We didn't need a wake-up call.

Elliot held my hand tight as we walked quietly along the river. For all the little things he'd griped about in the past, he wasn't complaining about this medical detour at all. We'll get through this, I thought, and we'll come out so much stronger.

The next morning we sat down with an elderly oncologist in Englewood. A jazz player in his spare time, he wore a green tweed jacket with a lime green shirt. His cuff links were circles with little green pig faces, perhaps a gift from a grandchild. I couldn't believe we were meeting on such a potentially momentous matter with a sax man in Porky cufflinks.

"It looks like pancreatic cancer," he said matter-of-factly, as he looked at Elliot's charts spread across his desk. "I know that's not what you wanted to hear."

I let out a whimper and tried to suck back the tears. I didn't mind crying but didn't want to fall apart. There was too much to try to understand. I leaned on Elliot's shoulder and he rubbed my leg as the oncologist went over various treatment options.

"A lot of lymph nodes are enlarged so surgery won't help for a cure," he added.

Elliot asked the question I didn't dare broach.

"So how much time are we talking about?"

"A year and a half, maybe two if you're very lucky."

Excuse me? Where did that come from? I hadn't the slightest idea things could be so grave. I'd seen many friends recover from breast cancer, so I had the impression that cancer in general had been tamed somewhat—especially for someone as young, strong and determined as Elliot. He was only fifty-five. We had barely begun our life together. There was no way it could be ripped away so soon. My world just didn't work that way—the naïf in me still believed that if you tried hard and did the right thing, life was supposed to be fair and decent and kind.

Elliot looked dazed. He took a big breath, let it out slowly and shook his head to clear the fog.

"Then again, I have one patient five years out," the oncologist offered, trying to throw us a morsel of hope. "There are exceptions for all rules about risks and predictions. You have to be like those Roman gladiators. You'd watch them in the movies and think how could they win? But some did."

He paused to let us absorb all this, and then repeated his advice.

"Be a gladiator."

We wandered outside, numb, and drove to a Teaneck hospital for yet another test, an endoscopic ultrasound. Finding the site of the primary tumor could affect the choice of chemotherapies. It would take an hour, so while Elliot was sedated I went downstairs to a quiet outdoor courtyard, pulled out my cell phone and called my parents at their house a few hours away in Sag Harbor.

As soon as my mother picked up the phone I broke down. Out came a primal keening wail. I couldn't stop. I hyperventilated. I could barely speak.

"I'm sorry," she said, bewildered. "I can't understand a word you're saying."

"They. Say. Elliot. Will. Be Lucky. To Live. Two years."

"Oh Honey, I'm so sorry." Her voice cracked. She paused. This news must have been a bolt out of nowhere. "Well, you'll just have to have as much fun and as many happy times as you can in the time you have left."

She passed the phone to my father.

"Poor Le," he said, using my childhood nickname. "It's just too tough. Too tough."

I could picture his hand kneading his forehead. "If there's anything we can do, we're here."

I felt so alone in that empty courtyard. I just stared dumbly at my phone. I could not stomach the notion I might have a longer relationship with my stupid 1994 Honda than with the love of my life.

After the procedure, the specialist announced he had finally found "the structure," a small offender—maybe three centimeters—in a very bad neighborhood. He drew a picture with a blue ballpoint pen.

As meticulous as I was about saving mementos, I had zero desire to keep that sketch.

Kate and Elliot at a Mets game, Fall 2006.

WIN THIS FOR MY BOYS
August 2006

Thanks to a last-minute cancellation, we got an 8:30 appointment the next morning at Memorial Sloan-Kettering Cancer Center. We were so anxious to make it that we got up at 5:00 a.m. to catch a train to New York. We arrived more than an hour too early.

"We could have taken a later train, but we weren't sleeping anyway," I rationalized.

"But I could lie there with you awake," Elliot replied. "That's even better."

That would have been swell. He always used that word, swell. I liked its old-fashioned Mayberry quality.

We could have used some extra rest. That first visit was a marathon. Sloan-Kettering always meant waiting around for hours and hours. Regulars knew to surrender the entire day. This place would be a wildly inconvenient choice for the long term, but Elliot wanted to be treated at the institution he saw as the gold standard.

When you got out of the elevator to the fourth-floor gastroenterology service, you saw a high desk manned by receptionists in dark blue jackets—most were very pretty girls in their twenties whose parents probably wished they'd go to grad school. After checking in, you walked into the wide waiting room that looked like a hotel lounge, with leathery couches and coffee tables full of magazines and daily flyers of new Sudoku puzzles.

The amenities aimed to keep anxious families from pestering the staff about what the hell was taking so damn long. On one end of the lounge sat two public computers with Internet access. On the other end stood the room where nurses took patients' blood before they saw the doctors as well as the hallway to the chemo infusion unit. That side had a pantry stocked with free sour balls, graham crackers, slim cans of apple juice (chilled and room temperature because some chemotherapies made patients oversensitive to cold drinks), tea and a coffee machine. The counter had a cheery cardboard sign from the eleventh-floor gift shop announcing the latest addition to their collection of Livestrong bracelets.

"New!" it chirped. "Purple for Pancreatic!"

Most of the lounge's widest wall was a huge window; you could see the bustle of Third Avenue below, all the cab drivers, pedestrians and scarf sellers on the corner oblivious to the terrified people watching them from above. There were dozens in the waiting room already, but often you couldn't tell who had cancer and who was family until you checked whose arm had a bandage from a blood draw. A few wore baseball caps or used a cane. One man kept spitting into pail. There was a striking Japanese woman with a chic black suit and a gorgeous head of glossy black hair. To my surprise she was called in for blood work. She didn't look sick at all. That was encouraging.

Cell phones rang, newspapers rustled, sick people hacked and coughed.

"Elliot Pinsley!" a receptionist shouted out. It was time to get his blood taken. In a move that would become our tender ritual, repeated countless times, Elliot put down his book, stood up, hoisted his drooping pants by the belt, leaned over and gave me a long, hard kiss on the lips before heading off. I was sending my gladiator into battle.

A chatty older woman seemed touched.

"The men usually come here with wives or girlfriends, but lots of women have to come on their own, or with a paid companion," she said. "If I were rich, I'd make sure every woman here went home with someone."

Just watch, I grumbled to myself. I'll take care of Elliot every step of the way, and then when it's my turn for chemo, I'll have to go it alone.

Hours passed before we were finally called in to see Dr. David Kelsen, the overtaxed head of the GI department. He was small and wiry, his sharp sparrow features masking deep compassion. He seemed all business in his long white lab coat, except for one lighthearted habit; after he washed his hands, he always wadded up the paper towel and tossed it into the garbage can across the room with a flick of the wrist like a basketball star.

After all that rushing to get to the city on time and hours of nerve-wracking anticipation, the consultation was woefully anti-climactic. Dr. Kelsen concurred with the sax man with the pig cufflinks—inoperable pancreatic cancer. Lucky to have a year or two. Conventional therapies were not very effective.

"It's a very difficult disease," he said soberly.

We had already booked a week at the beach with the kids later in August. Could we still take the trip?

"Certainly," he said. "Have a good time, get some rest and relax."

That was supposed to be the news we wanted to hear, but it sent another message: chemo wasn't likely to help that much, so there was no real hurry. We shuffled out feeling frazzled, deflated and weary to the core. But we'd only just begun.

We schlepped home on the train. This was the day we'd promised to take Alex to a Mets game for his tenth birthday. We'd given him the tickets back in June and didn't want to disappoint him. So after a futile attempt at a nap—we were too upset to sleep—we dragged ourselves into the car and fought rush hour traffic to get to Shea Stadium.

It felt surreal to be on the mezzanine on a beautiful summer night, smelling the hot dogs and popcorn and sweat, jumping up to see the best plays, cheering for the team Elliot had loved since he was about Alex's age. It turned out to be an exciting game.

Please, just win this for my boys, I begged silently. I felt like the mom in one of those cliché TV movies about a sick child whose dying wish is to see his team win the World Series. But this was real.

It happened to be the first time the Mets' hugely popular catcher, Mike Piazza, was playing again at Shea after switching to another team. When he sauntered onto the field the crowd erupted in deafening chants of "Mike Piazza! Mike Piazza!" They waved and waved and waved.

It felt like the whole stadium was waving goodbye. Goodbye to the good life that we worked so hard to build.

At least the Mets won that night.

WHAT TO SAY

How do you tell your children about this kind of cancer, the kind that can't be cured? And worse, perhaps, because sunny attempts at spin won't work, how do you tell a dying man's mother?

My brain was exploding with questions, each new one crowding out the last. It was easier to debate all the options in my head than to let myself feel anything. Do you tell them one by one so they can ask as much, or as little, as they want? Or do you gather them in a war room so they hear the news together and find some comfort in each other?

How would we manage the logistics anyway? Aaron, a jovial twenty-six-year-old, was in Chicago working as a computer trouble-shooter for a consortium that ran clinical trials for cancer drugs, of all things. There would be no whitewashing the statistics with him. Kate, settled with her boyfriend, Anthony, was selling juggling supplies over the Internet in New York. Max was packing for his freshman year at Ithaca College. Devon was in teen girl heaven at riding camp in Vermont. Alex was home with us, cheerfully bouncing around various baseball day camps.

How much of your fear do you let them see? What if you burst into tears?

My impulse, as usual, was to ask an expert. Defer to authority. Pass the buck for decision-making. There must be a right way to do this, I figured. It was just a matter of research, just like at my job. As if the phrasing or tone would really make a difference in the end.

I was so tense I couldn't wait until we could return to the city to get advice, so I scheduled a phone session right away for both of us with one of Sloan-Kettering's social workers, Carol. She was a round-faced, school-marmy woman we'd met briefly during our visit there.

When it was time for the three-way call, I perched tensely on my side of our bed, armed with a blue pen and my red notebook. Acting organized gave me delusions of control. Elliot sat Indian-style on his side, arched over his crossed legs, resting his forehead in one hand, staring at our mustard yellow quilt. We both held phones.

"Major in the truth," Carol advised us.

"What's that supposed to mean?" Elliot snapped. "My youngest son is just about to start college. How can he go off with this hanging over his head? My mother lost my father to cancer twenty years ago. How much is she supposed to take?"

It was clear he was taking out his frustration on this sixty-something counselor. Carol absorbed his anger. Guess she was used to it.

"Acknowledge to yourself that this is terrifying," she continued.

If you don't tell them soon, she warned, they'll find out anyway and you'll lose your credibility. They'll overhear you talking or see a medical bill in the mail. Tell each one alone because some may want lots of detail, others might not.

"Use age-appropriate language," she added. "The ten-year-old will keep asking questions until he's emotionally satisfied with the answers. When he stops asking, stop telling."

That sounded oddly like conventional guidance for telling children about sex.

"The children who need therapy later on are the ones who are isolated because information was kept from them," she went on. "Look out for eavesdropping. You want to be their first line of information. You want them to trust you. You don't have to go into all the scary statistics."

Elliot sounded testy as he worried aloud about dumping all this dark news on his three kids, who were just branching out into their young adult lives, and mine, who had, after years of two-steps-forward-one-step-back adjustment to living with a stepfather, finally come to feel so close to him.

"This is too much to ask them to handle," he insisted.

Carol told Elliot it would be wise to "come to terms with your own emotional response" to the diagnosis before telling the kids. He'll never come to terms with it, I thought. We can't wait that long.

"You need to be authentic when talking optimistically," she added. "You can say this is very hard, or this is very sad, and that you're starting treatment soon and hoping for the best."

In a few weeks we were supposed to go off on a family vacation to the beach in Cape May. Should we tell them before or after? Didn't the kids deserve one last lighthearted spree? She warned that our faces would betray us if we tried to keep this a secret. Especially since they knew Elliot had been seeing doctors for a lot of tests and he would be traveling with loads of pain pills.

"You can talk about it and then say let's take a break from the subject," she suggested.

What about Max? Elliot couldn't bear distracting him from what should be one of the most exciting new chapters of his life. And what if the ominous news took a toll on his work at college?

"Tell Max you want him to go off and have a wonderful time," she said. "You'll keep him posted if there's anything he needs know."

We hung up. Her practiced phrases made sense to me. It felt better to have a script. Elliot bristled. He thought she was patronizing.

For all his bluster, Elliot knew what we had to do. The reporter in him couldn't keep news to himself for long anyway. He told Aaron by phone, using a comfortable, casual, teddy bear tone totally unlike the hostile way he barked at the social worker. He said he'd be starting chemotherapy soon but didn't mention the grim outlook.

"Don't worry, kiddo," Elliot said. "I feel good, I'm strong and I don't give up. Your old man's tougher than you think."

He told Kate and Max much the same way. They absorbed the news quietly. They had their mother's stoic Wisconsin reticence. A few nights later, after Kate had dinner at our house, I drove her back to her boyfriend's apartment. I wanted to say something honest but encouraging. I talked to the windshield as we both stared straight ahead into the dark road ahead.

"This is hard, but Elliot's doing very well and we're lucky we live near the best treatment in the world," I said. "Just be careful about looking things up on the Internet. The statistics aren't great but Elliot doesn't really fit the profile. Most people who get this are older, or have Diabetes, or smoked a lot. He's young for this disease and he can do a lot better than most."

"Too late," she said. "I started checking all over the web and got hysterical. I knew I had to stop."

"Wise move."

Telling Alex took all of forty seconds. Elliot and I were lingering at breakfast with him when I plunged in. I'd been thinking back to those books I'd read a few years before about helping kids through divorce; they said children took their emotional cues from their parents, so I tried to sound relaxed and calm. I deserved an Oscar.

"Hey, Sweetie, you know how Elliot hasn't been feeling well?" I said. "Well, the doctors have done some tests and decided it's a kind of cancer, and he's going to start treatment soon."

"Whoah," said Alex. "I thought they said before that it wasn't cancer."

"Right, but then they did some more tests and they found out that it is. Some days he'll feel good and some days he probably won't because of the treatments."

"Oh," he said. "Okey dokey." And then he went off to watch some TV. That was it. For the moment anyway. His questions would come later, after months of percolating inside.

Devon was a different story. She was off at her favorite place in the world, a rambling farm in Vermont where a dozen girls rode horses, mucked out stalls and swam in a sparkling river to wash off their sweat. Once when we visited there was a pair of underwear dangling from a chandelier. Elliot called it "the commune." Devon adored it and I didn't want to wreck her final few days there. On our recent phone call she had been sulky, clearly pissed at me for saying Elliot and I couldn't drive up to get her when camp ended because of our work schedules. On the last day the girls showed off their riding and she wanted us to watch.

Devon's dad was picking her up instead. Milo considerately asked me what he should say if she wanted to know how Elliot was doing.

"I'd like to tell her myself if possible," I said, "but I don't want you to lie, so if you have to explain, go ahead."

Within minutes of getting into her father's car, Devon asked about Elliot. She wept through much of the six-hour drive home. As soon as they arrived, she bolted out of the car with a streaky red face, ran up our steps and threw her arms around my waist.

"I'm so sorry I gave you such a hard time about not coming to get me," she sobbed into my chest. "I didn't know Elliot was so sick. I feel so awful."

As wrenching as it was to see my child so devastated, I was touched. The intensity of her reaction was poignant proof of how much she had grown to love him. When she hugged Elliot long and tight, he was deeply moved. The other kids had been so much more reserved.

Elliot dreaded telling his mother. With a fluffy head of striking white hair, and fiercely proud to have all her own teeth in her eighties, Helen was a formidable whirlwind of energy, a self-appointed volunteer social worker who ran errands for her frail neighbors, buying them stamps, refilling their prescriptions, escorting them to doctors' appointments. She called them her "clients." All her serpentine sagas about her busy days led to points that were only tangentially related, and each account was punctuated by a repertoire of favorite phrases. "By the way." "I'll be honest with you." "As a matter of fact." "P.S" "I'm not like that." "I love her to death."

45

Helen was one-hundred-percent feistiness in sensible heels.

Elliot knew his diagnosis would crush her. He wouldn't tell her until we'd been back to Sloan-Kettering and had a battle plan in place so he could explain the treatment in the same breath as the illness.

The two of us went to see her for lunch. She was sitting straight-backed in a wicker armchair in her spotless one-bedroom apartment in Washington Heights when Elliot finally told her what was going on. Her long, angular face barely moved. She sat still as a stone. It was like she buckled on a metal coat of armor.

"I'm very upset," she said in a robotic monotone I'd never heard. "You know I've been through this before."

And as for me? I don't think I fully absorbed all this for months. I just tried to do what I had to do, one day a time, to keep us all going. I thought back on my days living near Mt. Fuji, where a Japanese friend worked grueling hours as a teacher, ran an immaculate household and raised three young children with little help. "Motherhood makes you strong," she used to say.

I was afraid to look far into the future. It was easier to focus on what to cook for dinner, when to schedule the next doctor's appointment, how to make sure we all had some fun together, and where Elliot and I could go for some invaluable time alone. I tried to cling to my own propaganda for the kids, that he was young and strong and didn't fit the profile of the grim statistics, but I didn't always fall for it. I had to be especially careful when I was in the car by myself. Any sad song on the radio could unhinge me. All the lyrics about loss and heartbreak—and that includes just about every song—seemed to be about us.

The Beatles' *In My Life* was a killer. "Out of all these friends and lovers, there is no one compared to you…."

A mournful ballad from the musical *Rent* unglued me too. "The earth turns, the sun burns, but I die without you…"

I had to turn off the music, wipe my tears and pull myself together. Crashing the car or losing my license was exactly what we didn't need.

Sometimes I could keep the darkest thoughts at bay.

Sometimes I couldn't, and would feel overwhelmed by a shadow of loneliness to come.

Sometimes I even tried to imagine what it would feel like to lose my husband, as if enduring the emptiness in advance would vaccinate me against the day it actually came. Then I would force myself to stop such self-flagellation.

He's here now, I told myself. You'll have plenty of time to mourn him later. Get as close to him as you can, while you can.

One such moment hit a few nights after Elliot's diagnosis. We were at Taro, a casual but elegant French-Asian fusion restaurant where you could eat outside on the sidewalk at bistro tables with candles and tiny vases of pink flowers. We were tired but relaxed after a packed day of tennis, a picnic in Central Park and a softball game back home with a group of Montclair writers. It seemed like Elliot was trying to jam a lifetime into the two weeks before chemo started.

We sat quietly, holding hands on the tabletop, glad to be so at ease that we could sit together without talking much. I couldn't help eavesdropping on the thirty-something pair at the next table. They were clearly on a first date, all awkward jokes and forced laughter. He was bald and nebbishy with black-rimmed glasses and smooth baby cheeks. She looked tense and bony, nervously flicking the end of her tight ponytail. He tried to engage her with tales about his nutritionist; she professed awe at his ability to resist chocolate; and each kept asking the other about how their date was going so far. After going round and round about what to order, they ended up with the safest bet, mango chicken.

It was excruciating to witness.

How awful it is to be them, I thought, so lonely and single and desperate for connection. How much better it is to be us.

Please please please don't let me end up back where they are, I begged some invisible power I wished I could believe in. I finally have the man I want. It's way too soon to lose him.

Let us enjoy this time together. We are here now. Let us just be.

THE THINGS I CARRIED

I had a thick spiral notebook with a tough red plastic jacket. I called it my cancer bible. The inside covers were taped full of business cards from Elliot's growing team of doctors. Keeping scrupulous records gave me a purpose, a sense that I was helping and the thin illusion of influence. The first fifty or so pages showed my hasty but meticulous notes on Elliot's symptoms, doctors' visits and drugs' side effects. When he started daily chemo pills plus weekly infusions in the city, with one week off every month, I scribbled down all the information, even the nurse's tip about a cheap garage.

All that detail came from the very start of our ordeal. As time went on, I just used the red book as a folder and shoved dozens of accumulating handouts into the back—advice on what to feed a patient who can no longer digest fat, a "pain management instruction sheet," and so on.

There was also a pale orange card about "Sexuality, Fertility and Intimacy" during treatment. We didn't need that one. Elliot had plenty of passion for what we referred to as "marital activities," using the phrase of a shy doctor who had granted us permission to "resume" them after Elliot healed from an invasive procedure.

"Shall we resume some marital activities?" one of us would whisper with a mischievous touch and a grin. Elliot said such pleasures were the best distraction from his daily discomforts and fears and phone hassles over prescriptions. They made him feel alive. Our bed was the one place he could come close to feeling carefree again. I tried to be a nurse by day and a vixen by night, and his lavish attentions made me feel safe and treasured. I have few regrets about how we managed during his illness but this is one; sometimes I was just too exhausted. If only I could have those nights back. What I would give for that chance.

My cancer bible also held artifacts from the parallel track of normal family life—a calendar for concerts at the Cloisters, a random to-do list ("plumber, birthday present, take Devon to riding on Friday"), and phone numbers I needed for work.

People often imagine that if they get hit by a terminal diagnosis they'd quit their jobs and fly to Tahiti. That's not usually the case. Like many patients, Elliot had to keep working for the paycheck and health insurance. More than that, work gave him a sense of identity and purpose. He didn't want to sit on the sidelines, he wanted to contribute. Quitting would mean admitting he didn't have much time left. Ironic, how the work he once grumbled about became so precious. Our jobs became lifelines. Our offices gave us diversions, time with friends and news to talk about that had nothing to do with doctors. Work preserved, as much as possible, some of the most basic rhythms of ordinary life. It was a blessing that our employers were flexible about our schedules, and that Elliot had an editing job he could do from home when need be.

For some reason, perhaps the satisfaction of private vengeance, my red bible also had a page I ripped out of a waiting room magazine. The article was titled "How Cancer Made a Mother Out of Me." The author veered from self-pity to celebration as she beat breast cancer and gloated about the wonderful lessons learned; I resented her weepy tale of triumph, knowing that Elliot almost certainly wouldn't be a winner.

One particularly in-your-face quotation caught my eye. It was in her doctor's riff about doing a breast cancer walk-a-thon. "'They couldn't have a pancreatic cancer walk,' he said. 'Almost no one survives pancreatic cancer.'"

My reaction screamed across the author's smiling head shot.

"BITCH!" I had scrawled in block letters over her bright green eyes, her shiny coral lipstick, her careful blond highlights. "FUCK YOU!"

That's how I vented my fury. On secret pieces of paper stashed in special hiding places. I didn't want anyone to see how hopeless I really felt. I had always told Elliot everything, but this I couldn't share. I was afraid if he saw my despair, he would give up. I wanted him to fight as hard as he could.

I needed him.

Every day brought new reminders. Once I drove to baseball camp to pick up Alex. As he opened the car door and buckled his seat belt, he seemed to be choking back tears.

"What's wrong, Honey?"

"Nothing."

"Are you sure?"

He was silent as we drove home. A few hours later, Alex spoke up.

"When they were picking teams, I got picked fifteenth out of eighteen."

"Oh, Honey, I'm so sorry." I couldn't think of anything else to say. I'm not a sports person. It seemed there was no way to spin this so it wouldn't hurt quite so much. This was a big part of a little boy's world, and I felt totally inept. It killed me to see Alex so despondent.

"Don't worry about it kiddo," Elliot said when he heard about it later. "It happens to everybody at some point. Mike Piazza got picked last in the sixty-second round of the 1988 amateur draft. More than a thousand guys got picked before him and he got drafted only as a favor because his dad knew somebody."

Alex's face lit up. Of course Elliot knew exactly what to say.

How was I going to raise my son without him?

LAST KISSES
October 2006

How many times can you kiss your husband for the last time?

How many times can you bear the crushing weight of thinking this might really be the end?

And let me ask you this: If you're kissing him, but he's too drugged to know it, or unconscious, does it count as a final kiss?

Elliot had one high-tech procedure after another—stents and drains and filters placed deep inside—and every time they wheeled him away for sedation I wondered if this moment would be our last. Doctors called these procedures "minimally invasive" but there was always a risk of complications, and each new step seemed like more of a medical high-wire act than the one before. And Elliot, who hated being alone, had to go into those sterile, shiny operating rooms without me. Our fervent goodbye kisses, with desperate see-you-when-you-wake-up smiles, depleted me. Each one had to be memorable enough to last a lifetime, just in case.

As soon as the heavy operating room doors swung shut behind his gurney and I had to turn away, my chin would quiver, my eyes would well up and I would head off in a shaky daze to cry, or call his mother who was no doubt staring at her phone, or page through a magazine about clothes I'd never wear or food I'd never cook, or I'd walk downstairs to the clattering grey cafeteria that smelled like old beef broth to get some breakfast, even though my mouth would be sandpaper dry and I could barely swallow.

Our first last kiss came in October, two months after Elliot's diagnosis.

We weren't yet resigned to the reality that we had to act on every clue from his embattled body. He'd gotten oddly short of breath during a walk in the woods, but Aaron was visiting for the weekend, and Devon had a horseshow on Sunday, and Elliot didn't want to miss the fun.

But Monday morning he woke up with serious chest pains. When we called the doctor said get to the nearest ER. I rushed us to a hospital in Teaneck that I gambled would take us quickly. It turned out there were blood clots in Elliot's lungs. He was whisked straight to the Intensive Care Unit

Hour after hour ticked by. Elliot had more trouble breathing, and the pain got worse. An IV dripped morphine into one arm and he drifted in and out of fitful sleep. An oxygen mask over his nose made his face sweat. I paced. Night fell. His breathing grew more labored, his head lolled from side to side. A young black-haired doctor kept coming in, his brow furrowed. It looked like this was more than a rookie could handle. I didn't really trust him but had little choice. Elliot was clearly suffering but the doctor worried that more morphine would depress his breathing too much.

"Mr. Pinsley," the doctor said, peering into Elliot's faraway, unfocused eyes. "Mr. Pinsley, how are you feeling? Mr. Pinsley. Can you hear me?"

He didn't respond to little slaps on his cheek. The doctor turned to me.

"One option is to intubate him to help him breathe. That would let his body rest."

Are you kidding me? I thought. It's this dire already? We just started…

"Is that like a ventilator?" I asked.

"Yes."

"But if you put him on a ventilator, will he get off? Is it temporary?"

"That's hard to say."

"What's the percentage? What percent of people who are put on a respirator are taken off?"

"It depends. Let me call his cardiologist for a consult."

The doctor left the room. It was two in the morning. The sky was black through the window. I saw my reflection in the glass, alone, holding a blanket tight around my shivering shoulders. I was terrified and kicking myself. I should have taken him to New York. This wouldn't be happening at Sloan-Kettering. They'd know what to do.

The young doctor came back, saying the cardiologist agreed he should intubate, if I agreed.

But how was I supposed to know what to do? When you talk about a living will over coffee in the lawyer's office, it's simply not the same. The papers we signed in there, back when everything seemed clear cut, didn't seem relevant. We had parsed out the opaque language—no heroic measures if there was no chance for recovery to a meaningful life—but this doctor didn't know if Elliot would ever get off the machine once he got on. He couldn't predict what kind of life Elliot might wake up to, if he woke up. All I knew was that once you get hooked up, it's agonizing for a family to unhook you.

I'd thought about this a lot. Years earlier I had visited the parents of Karen Ann Quinlan for an interview about the landmark court decision that let Karen die, finally, after she lingered for years on machines in an irreversible coma. I always swore if I ever ended up in that hopeless condition I'd want to be taken off life support. In fact, I'd deliberately neglected to update my health care proxy, leaving my first husband in charge. Elliot wouldn't pull the plug on me.

Clearly, you don't want to get on a breathing machine unless it's absolutely necessary, and this doctor didn't have enough information for such a critical decision. It was 2:30 a.m. All this seemed so hasty and haphazard.

But how could I do nothing? Elliot was a fighter. He'd want the chance to try to beat his way back. And if he couldn't wake up, if I would be forced to decide for him that an unthinking, unfeeling, unchanging life was not worth living, then that would be my burden.

"Okay," I told the doctor tentatively. "Do it, I guess."

I leaned over and kissed Elliot's hot forehead so many times. Then I lifted off the mask, for just a minute, please, and kissed his mouth. Then his forehead again. It was slick and salty. What if this kiss is our last, or this one? He wouldn't even know we had it. Just one more, please. Then I forced myself to pull away, afraid to take too long, and willed my feet to walk into the quiet corridor. I didn't want to see what the doctor was about to do.

My body crumpled into a grey plastic chair by the nurses' station. I collapsed into sobs so fierce I couldn't breathe. My heart pounded so fast and my chest heaved so hard my ribs ached.

"Are you okay?" a nurse asked.

No words could come out. It felt like I was drowning, like the time I fell into the violence of the rapids on a rafting trip in Idaho. I'd lost my balance in a little yellow rubber kayak and got sucked under freezing water, water that was hurtling between rocks and whirlpools and crashing foam. The guide had said never put your feet down, they'll get stuck and anchor you to the ground and the water will rush over you and flatten you and drown you even if it's just a few inches deep. So I tried to curl up with my knees and hold my breath as the current trapped me under the kayak, my life jacket forcing me up into its bottom. Then the river spat me out, dragged me under again and yanked me around until I didn't know which way was up. If I panic now I will die. Desperate to breathe, almost faint, I couldn't last another second when a strong arm grabbed me and swooped my head and shoulders onto the front of his kayak. I gulped in air with deep groans. Suddenly we were someplace calm. My legs dangled limp.

Now a nurse grabbed me under the armpits and pulled me into the empty family lounge and sat me down on a soft couch. Her arm was around my shoulder, she said it would be okay, don't worry, try to breathe.

But what if this was it, so soon, how would I tell his mother, how would I tell the kids? I couldn't believe I was already a hysterical wife, about to be a widow.

The door to the lounge burst open. Another nurse rushed in.

"Your husband woke up when they were starting with the tube. He said no, he didn't want it. He wants to see you now."

"He said no?" I repeated dumbly. "Is he okay?"

"Come see him," she said.

And there he was, looking at me. I thought I had lost him, but he was back, and I had never seen his eyes look into mine with such searching. I kissed him again, and again, and again.

MY KIND OF FAITH

Elliot stayed in intensive care, hooked up to oxygen and intravenous medicines, drifting in and out of a morphine haze. After several tense days, a nurse named Lisa pulled me aside.

"The only way Elliot will find peace," she said, "is through God."

That stung. I resented her assumption he needed to find faith if he was going to have comfort. We wanted to put our trust in doctors, not help from above. Surely she shouldn't have said such a thing. Even in a Catholic hospital, staff was supposed to respect everyone's point of view. I wondered if I should report Lisa's transgression to her boss.

Her prescription haunted me. We weren't religious, and I couldn't help thinking that if I had been, seeing Elliot suffer this way would have shattered my faith altogether. If there was a God, I told myself, he was doing a shitty job and I wanted nothing to do with him.

Of course it wasn't necessary to go through a personal medical crisis to see injustice on the alleged Almighty's watch. Every day the newspaper displayed the slaughter of innocents through wars, fires and earthquakes, but seeing Elliot's pain up close brought the issue to the forefront for me. I wanted to understand what support people got from religion, and how they could keep their convictions under such duress. It occurred to me I had never really talked with my friends about faith. Like sex lives and bank accounts, it was something personal that we just didn't probe in detail.

And so, for the first time in my life, I began to ask. Some people told me they found God an indispensable pillar during an illness. Some experienced a spiritual awakening. A few gave up on faith altogether, while others fought to keep it alive. I was a bit jealous of those who believed in heaven; the idea you could rejoin your soul mate in an eternal afterlife certainly made death seem less daunting. I didn't believe I'd have that chance. In my view, we had only the here and now, and had to make the very best of it. Religion came into my life only as an excuse for warm family meals at Christmas, Easter, Rosh Hashana and Passover.

I contacted the pastoral care department at Holy Name Hospital in Teaneck, where Elliot was, as he put it, "incarcerated." Sister Lois Jablonski said some patients became so furious at God that they kicked her out of the room. A few were tortured by the terrifying idea they got sick as retribution for their sins. She said God didn't punish that way.

"There's no answer to the question, 'Why did I get cancer?'" she said simply. "I just try to stay with the person and listen to him vent his feelings and not make any judgments."

To me that wasn't a very satisfying response. I found myself bristling at the fact that some people gave God credit for the good in the world but didn't hold him responsible for the bad. They said God didn't micromanage. Then why pray for specifics, like recovery or a new job or a baby?

The whole issue made me cranky. Once a priest on the pastoral care team stopped by Elliot's room to see if there was anything he could do to help.

"Sure," I snapped. "Can you turn up the heat?"

I knew I was being peevish and unfair. Yes, the perversion of religion had fueled terrorists and other crazies, but I had also witnessed its benevolence. As a reporter I had met dozens of foster parents. Most of the best ones were devout Christians whose faith inspired amazing self-sacrifice.

One day, as Elliot and I were taking one of his first tentative strolls around the hallways of the Teaneck hospital to rebuild his strength, we heard a bunch of giggles in the stairwell. Out popped a half a dozen teenage boys in yarmulkes. They looked around a bit and came up to us.

"Mr. Pinsley?" one asked timidly.

"Yes," he answered.

"Good Shabbas!" they said in cheerful cacophony. Then they ran off.

Elliot got a huge kick out of that. Apparently he was a stop on their "mitzvah" tour of good deeds. He must have checked off the Jewish box when he was admitted.

"They knew who I was by my nose," he said.

I was grateful those boys gave Elliot a laugh, a welcome feeling of fellowship and a funny story to tell. I had deep respect for the community service mission of many faiths. Nevertheless, I couldn't understand religious explanations for sufferings that are blatantly unfair.

As I asked around, people kept telling me to check out a book called *When Bad Things Happen to Good People.* Somehow everybody seemed to have read it.

The author, Rabbi Harold S. Kushner, wrote it to make sense of the devastating loss of his son, Aaron, who was only fourteen when he died of a rare genetic disorder. At first the rabbi expresses outrage at a God who allows terrible accidents and disease to strike the undeserving. He questions whether he can keep teaching that a merciful God watches over the world. Ultimately he concludes that God doesn't cause tragedies, but can provide the tools people need to persevere.

"The ability to forgive and the ability to love are the weapons God has given us to enable us to live fully, bravely and meaningfully in this less-than-perfect world," he writes.

Well, okay, forgiveness and love were values I could subscribe to. I just didn't need the God part.

While I didn't want anyone to tell me what to believe, it always touched me when friends told us we were in their prayers. I understood that was their way of expressing they cared. One thoughtful stranger who heard about Elliot's condition even sent me a hand-crocheted "prayer shawl." I never used it for worship, but her generosity moved me. There was so much compassion around us. That was something I could believe in. Human kindness helped me keep going.

By the end of Elliot's ten days in the hospital, I decided not to file a complaint about the nurse who sent me on these philosophical wanderings because she did such a great job with her professional duties. She was attentive and exacting.

At one point she handed Elliot a clear plastic toy with a little blue ball inside. He was supposed to exercise his lungs by blowing into it to make the ball rise as high as possible. The sheer effort hurt so much he grimaced. He kept pressing the red button that dosed him with morphine.

"Blow into the toy ten times every hour," Lisa said. "And try to lay off the pain medicine. You're using quite a lot."

She meant business. Elliot blew into that toy every few minutes. He never pushed that morphine button again. His discipline amazed me. He was putting himself through hell in hopes he could heal faster and come home.

Watching him gave me more strength than a prayer ever could. If he could endure this torture, I thought, I could hang in there with him. He called me his "ER angel."

I kept that toy as a reminder of his determination to do everything in his power to do something as simple as breathe. Now the toy is dusty and cracked, but to me it is a symbol of grace.

MY GUIDES TO THE WILDERNESS

After Elliot came home we had a peaceful Thanksgiving, but I craved a clearer picture of what might come next. There had to be someone who could give me a clue, or at least help me handle the unexpected. I looked for guidance almost everywhere.

I asked a social worker at Sloan-Kettering if she knew any counselors near me who helped families facing cancer. She handed me a long list of specialists. Two had offices in Montclair.

The one named Lissa Parsonnet called me back first. She must have heard desperation in my voice because she shifted her schedule to squeeze me in.

Lissa was stylish, petite and fit with a full head of curly blond hair. At fifty, she ran a marathon and went zip-lining in Costa Rica. Her radiant skin and enthusiasm struck me as the polar opposite of the disease she had devoted her career to discussing. I don't know how she could listen to so many bleak stories, but she loved her job and it showed.

Her cozy third-floor office had a soft couch and endless boxes of tissues.

"I'm so damn tired," I complained.

At home I was trying to look calm, sure and strong, but in Lissa's office I let myself blubber like a baby. I poured out my worries that my kids felt shunted aside when I bolted off to deal with Elliot's emergencies. I whined that I never got a minute to relax. I demanded to know how this mess would unfold. How could I tell the difference between a temporary setback and the beginning of the end?

"Everyone's always talking about hope, how you have to have hope," I wailed as I soaked yet another tissue in tears. "How am I supposed to be hopeful when I know he's going to die?"

"Hope can change," Lissa said.

"What do you mean?"

"At first you hope he gets better. If there's no cure you hope he lives for a long time. Then for a good quality of life. Then you hope for comfort. Then for a peaceful death."

"That's awfully depressing."

It was a relief to admit that. With Lissa I could talk about death in a way I didn't dare with Elliot. He just couldn't face the subject and I would never force him to. I was too busy to see her more than once every month or two, but when I did go it was cathartic and liberating. I'd pull one Kleenex after another out of her tidy plastic box, mop my face, blow my nose, stuff each tissue into my clenched fist and then hurl the snotty wad into the wastebasket at my feet.

"What are you doing to take care of yourself?" she always asked. "What are you doing for balance?"

It was gratifying to hear somebody give me permission, even encouragement, to take a break. Her voice was low, soothing and sincere. Sometimes I felt like I was paying her just to tell me not to be so hard on myself. I would do anything to hear someone besides Elliot tell me I was doing a good job, that I had a right to feel this whole ordeal was unfair and that it was okay to worry about myself too. I had some good friends I could talk to, and I did sometimes, but I didn't want all my conversations with them to be downers and I didn't want to act self-centered. It's okay to be self-absorbed in a counselor's office. That's the whole point.

When I left Lissa's office my upper lip would be sore from all those tissues and I'd be spent, yearning to sleep. Sometimes I did. Then I'd get up, make dinner and get back to the grind. By then my breathing was a little deeper, my shoulders a bit less tense, my path a little clearer.

Books were another source of solace. I read *The Human Side of Cancer* by Dr. Jimmie C. Holland, who pioneered the study of the psychological issues faced by families affected by the disease. Her book helped me understand the existential trials confronting Elliot, but out of 344 pages, only eighteen focused on the caregiver's experience—plus one grim final chapter on bereavement.

What was most helpful was the way Holland explained the deeply human need to find meaning in our lives. She quoted Viktor Frankl, a Viennese psychiatrist:

"Even a man who finds himself in great distress. . . can still give his life a meaning by the way he faces his fate, his distress, by taking his unavoidable suffering upon himself. Life holds a meaning for each and every individual, and even more, it retains this meaning to his last breath. Life never ceases to have a meaning."

Frankl wrote this manuscript, *The Doctor and the Soul*, before being hauled off to the concentration camp at Auschwitz. He rewrote it after World War II. That certainly got me thinking. At least Elliot's suffering was not inflicted by another man's evil.

Still, where was the meaning in it?

I couldn't find any purpose in hunting for a miracle cure. That project seemed doomed to fail. I wanted to focus on something achievable, and, after chewing on this for a while, realized I could invest meaning in anything I wanted. It was my personal meaning, my value, my choice. What I wanted was as deep a connection to my husband as I could get. Nothing could stop me from finding meaning in our marriage, in how we treated each other and how we shaped memories for our family. If we did our best to show our children how to face life's greatest hardships with courage and devotion, that would matter. Even his death could not take that away.

Although at times it was hard to focus on something so abstract—when car repairs or laundry or work deadlines devoured a day—this mission was something clear that I could keep coming back to. Its power was bolstered every time we said "I love you," and we said that all the time.

What Remains was another eye-opener. It was Carole Radziwill's memoir of taking care of her husband, Anthony, as he underwent a relentless series of surgeries for cancer that spread to his lungs. They were young, in love and working in journalism, and with that I could certainly relate. I turned the pages with admiration as she described how her indefatigable husband bounced back from one medical crisis after another. It was a star-studded story: Anthony was great friends with his glamorous cousin, John F. Kennedy Jr., who had made the whole country weep as he saluted his father's funeral procession. John's gorgeous wife, Carolyn Bessette, was Carole's closest friend.

The four of them dined together, went on luxurious vacations and celebrated milestones with bottomless champagne. As Anthony got sicker and treatments stopped working, Carole tried to cherish their final days up in Martha's Vineyard. John and Carolyn were on their way to visit when their plane crashed into the Atlantic Ocean. This fairy tale prince from Camelot, who apparently made a grave mistake as a pilot, vanished into the water along with his wife and her sister.

Just when Carole was focusing all her might on keeping her husband alive, death hit their closest friends. Tragedy struck when she was looking the other way.

What a cautionary tale. It made me think again about the urgency of tending to my children. What if, while I was busy pouring all my energy into Elliot, something happened to them? I couldn't live with that. Such an agonizing prospect added a new world of pressure to the struggle to give everyone in my house enough attention, but I was glad for the warning.

I didn't want to look only at cancer books for wisdom. Any example of resilience would do.

Among the best was *Infidel* by Ayaan Hirsi Ali. She must be one of the bravest women on the planet. Raised in a strict Muslim family in Somalia, she survived female mutilation, beatings and civil war. She ran away from an arranged marriage by escaping to the Netherlands, where she put herself through college, became a Parliament member and fought for the rights of Muslim women. Religious extremists threatened to kill her so she fled again, this time to America. Her courage was truly amazing, and she was so alone. At least I could take comfort in my family and friends. If she could overcome the incredible adversities in her life, I figured, I could handle mine.

As time went on, I soaked up inspiration from a wider range of sources. Anything could apply—Chinese fortune cookies, letters to the editor and song lyrics. One blues singer, Vivian Greene, had a great and famous line: "Life is not about waiting for the storm to pass," she sang. "It's about learning to dance in the rain."

One of my favorites came from the tag on a Celestial Seasonings teabag.

"Choose well," it advised. "Your choice is brief, and yet endless."

"Who said that?" I quizzed Elliot.

"I don't know," he shrugged. "Yoda?"

"No, Goethe."

We laughed. I still carry that teabag tag in my wallet. The memory of that goofy banter always makes me smile. A sense of humor can be key to survival.

ADVENTURES IN WEED
December 2007

Elliot was shedding weight at an alarming pace. He'd lost forty pounds since flying to Italy nearly six months earlier. One day his doctors quietly advised him to try an unofficial route to an appetite.

Medical marijuana.

It was illegal in New Jersey, but Elliot liked the idea. He thought it might ease the anxieties that had begun to plague him. It's hard to relax when every week you're confronted with your mortality up close at the chemo clinic.

"I don't think I'll ever feel carefree again," he told me.

And so I added "get pot" to my growing to-do list.

That was definitely new territory. I grew up a complete goodie-goodie. Cigarettes never had any appeal. I'd tried a joint once in college but the smoke burned my throat and I had zero interest in ever trying again.

That's why I found it amusing that it became my job to procure the cannabis. Somehow Elliot's buddies, who came of age on college campuses rocking with sex, drugs and the anti-war protests of the early 1970s, didn't come through. They'd cut their hippie ponytails long ago.

My women friends, masters at juggling jobs, carpools and book clubs, were much more efficient. As soon as I dropped a hint, three of them stepped right up.

The first was a tennis player who seemed quite well connected. A few nights after she learned what I needed we stood in her kitchen, where a huge blackboard was covered with color-coded block letters in pink and green chalk detailing her children's afterschool activities. She handed me a white legal envelope embossed with a Merrill Lynch logo.

"How much does it cost?" I asked in wonder.

"It's a gift," she said. "There's more where that came from if you need it."

I tucked it in my purse and drove the ten blocks home slowly, peering cautiously over the steering wheel, afraid to attract the slightest attention lest I get pulled over with my cache. I felt like an undercover operator, a bad girl, a spy. It was actually a bit of a thrill. Amazing, what we do for love.

I thought of saving the package for Elliot's Christmas present but was too excited to wait. He was taking a shower when I got home. I burst into the bathroom and pulled open the curtain.

"You'll never guess what I have," I exclaimed.

"What?" he asked.

"Look!" I dangled the envelope.

He leaned over and sniffed it.

"Oy vey," he said, somewhat stunned. Then he grinned, dripping wet, and pulled me halfway into the shower for a big kiss that left me half-soaked. "That's my girl."

The second source came through a few days later. She had just confiscated some contraband from under her sixteen-year-old son's pillow.

"Better you should have it than him," she said as she passed me a bud in a teeny baggie the size of a postage stamp. We couldn't believe a publicly traded company manufactured a product that seemed designed expressly for this purpose. It made Elliot uncomfortable to benefit from a high school black market but that supplier didn't last anyway. Pretty soon the boy got busted, spent a night in jail and realized getting a record might wreck his college application.

The third source's husband was part of a monthly poker game of journalists. One knew somebody who knew somebody. That delivery smelled positively rank, but it was particularly potent.

The ban on medical marijuana infuriated me. I fantasized about daring New Jersey politicians to look my bony husband in the eye and tell him exactly why he couldn't relish a little reefer to alleviate his roiling stomach. If a child got hold of the OxyContin and other prescription painkillers floating freely around his knapsack, the results would be far more dangerous. Even deadly. The only people to benefit from the stupid law were the smugglers, dealers and gangs who got rich trading it underground. Many would be defanged if patients could grow their own or obtain it legally.

As much as the prohibition enraged me, it didn't seem wise to teach my kids by example that it's okay to break laws you disdain. They used to come home from middle school health classes to regale me with nightmare accounts of teenagers who escalated from weed to hard-core narcotics. Little did they know of the plastic baggies full of pot upstairs in mommy's bedroom.

To keep the stuff out of harm's way I got a lockbox from Costco. It was grey, heavy and fireproof, about the size of a toaster. As long as I'd bothered to buy it, I figured I might as well use it to protect our important documents as well, our wills, birth certificates and passports.

"Great idea," Elliot said with a chuckle when I proudly presented him with the key. "But do you really want to get to customs at the airport with a passport that smells like pot?"

Damn. I raced to rescue all the paperwork and flapped it wildly in the air to neutralize the scent.

We tried to be careful when he smoked. At first he did it only when the kids were spending the night at friends' houses or their dad's. Then we got a bit looser and he indulged only when they were asleep. Then when they were upstairs doing homework. Not so smart.

One night Elliot was smoking while we watched a movie on TV. Devon flung open the doors.

"What smells like shit?" she demanded.

I was so eager for her to leave I didn't scold her for cursing.

"Oh, some herbal remedy Elliot's trying," I replied, fanning away the haze like a wayward teenager caught by the rents.

"It's really awful," she declared as she stomped away. "Yuck."

It was a close call but satisfying as well; her unfamiliarity with the smell suggested she had no experience with it herself.

In 2010 New Jersey became the fourteenth state to approve medical marijuana. I wish Elliot could have seen that day. My kids asked whether he ever used it. I thought for a moment about what to tell them, and then decided on the truth. They had grown up enough to understand that under certain rare, carefully examined circumstances, you have to break the rules to do the right thing.

INSTA-NURSE
January 2007

My Christmas present to Elliot was a pair of plane tickets to Captiva, Florida, for Martin Luther King Day weekend. I wanted to celebrate making it through a half-year of treatment. But a few days before our flight, Elliot's eyes turned yellow as a tiger's and he got hit by debilitating waves of nausea. I begged him to let me take him to the ER. He was too miserable to get out of bed. He was just rolling on the sweat-drenched sheets, clutching his stomach, moaning. I threatened to call an ambulance to get him to move. He didn't want all that drama so he finally relented and hobbled into the car.

I raced like a NASCAR driver into the city, zooming in and out of lanes and rolling down my window to wave cars out of my way. It was impossible to avoid the potholes. Every bump sent Elliot into a massive groan. He clutched a brown paper grocery bag I'd lined with white plastic. As soon as we got to the ER he retched into it with violent heaves.

"He has an obstruction," a pretty young doctor concluded after some quick tests. A backup of bile had caused his jaundice. She was going to put a tube down his nose to get out the gunk that was stuck behind the blockage.

"Is this going to be horrible?" Elliot asked.

"Well, I won't lie," she replied. "It's not going to be that comfortable. But it will only take a minute."

A nurse whipped the beige curtain closed around his bed and asked me to step outside. I paced in the hall, my arms crossed hard. Then came the most agonized groan of them all, a guttural cry of shock. Dear God. Please let that be the last. My sweet man really doesn't deserve such torture. A guilt pang hit too—I knew that if that primal roar had come from my child, I would wish it could be me in that bed instead. But it was coming from an adult, I felt lucky to be on the safe side of the curtain, and I was disgusted at my selfish impulse for self-protection. For all the times I resented the fact that Elliot couldn't fathom my sadness—the pain of knowing that I would be left alone, forced to build a new life without him—here was a reminder that I couldn't truly know his physical agonies and sense of dread.

Mercifully, Elliot felt better within minutes. He stayed in the hospital for five days, cracking jokes about what it said about his nose that he had a bigger nasal-gastric tube than anybody else on the unit. Those poor souls looked like depressed elephants as they plodded up and down the hallways with those long appendages hanging from bandaged nostrils. I wanted to remember how brave he'd been so I took a cell phone photo of Elliot. It's the only shot he ever objected to.

He also had a new tube protruding from his side. It drained clear amber bile into a plastic bag strapped to his leg. It reminded me of the bag attached to the disabled soldier played by Jon Voigt in *Coming Home*. To my surprise, doctors said Elliot would be coming home with the ugly thing. And it would be my job to take care of it.

Oy. I am squeamish. Once when I was little I fainted when my puppy got a shot. Even now I cover my eyes when a scalpel flashes before a surgery scene in a hospital drama. I couldn't bear to watch my son wiggle a loose tooth.

And yet I was forced to become an insta-nurse.

I had to learn to clean and dress this sore, alien wound under Elliot's ribcage. It looked like a bullet hole, raw and pink and oozy. On the very day I thought I would be sifting through sand hunting for seashells with him on a romantic getaway, I was trembling in the face of this icky new responsibility.

Fortunately our favorite hospital nurse, Daniella, was dispatched to Elliot's hospital room to teach me what to do. She was chatty and upbeat as she fussed with scissors and tape and foam pads.

"Think of it as an arts and crafts project," Elliot told me cheerfully, just glad to be on our way home. "You're really good at those."

The wound wasn't supposed to get wet so every time Elliot took a shower, I had to tape plastic all over his chest to keep out water. It was like the reverse of *The Total Woman*, that 1970s marriage manual that encouraged wives to greet their husbands at the front door after a long workday dressed in nothing but Saran Wrap. This getup wasn't exactly sexy.

It is astonishing what you can get used to. Even joke about.

"The search for the perfect drainage bag goes on," Elliot emailed me one day after he'd gone back to work, hiding his new accoutrement under his clothes. The only model in the pharmacy had six feet of tubing. "I don't think I could fit that in my pants. I don't think a defensive tackle for the Giants could fit that in his pants."

Then came another shocker.

I had to pull a three-quarter-inch needle out of Elliot's upper chest. The very idea made me sweat.

"It's easy," said the sunny nurse named Lorna. She had a big wide smile and an island lilt in her voice.

"I dunno," I said warily. "I'm not good with needles."

That bile obstruction had signaled the first combination of chemotherapies had stopped working; the new plan called for drugs that required my hands-on assistance at home disconnecting a chemo pump. I was trying not to panic—about this unnerving new nursing assignment as well as the tumor's spread.

Dr. Kelsen was frank in reminding us that no drugs had great success against the aggressive growth of pancreatic cancer. "A handful of people respond well to certain therapies for a while," he said, "and you might be one of the fortunate few." It seemed he didn't want to get our hopes up but he didn't want to dash them either.

Focus on near term, I told myself. And there was one bright side: the new treatment required exhausting schleps to the city only twice a month, instead of three times.

The new pair of drugs had to be infused slowly, one teaspoon per hour over the course of two days. That meant Elliot had to come home from the clinic wearing the pump. It was about the size of a baby bottle and fit into a pouch that hung on his belt.

It was a clever invention. A thin tube from the bottle was attached to a needle inserted into that "port" implanted near Elliot's collarbone. The writer Lorrie Moore aptly likened the device to Frankenstein's bolt. The other end of the tube was connected to the bottle-sized pump holding a yellow balloon full of medicine. As the balloon shrank the drug was slowly squeezed into Elliot's bloodstream.

One of the drugs was known as 5-FU. When the nurse announced it would be my job to detach the pump at home, my reaction was absolutely FU.

I wanted nothing to do with pulling a needle out of my husband.

"Okay, I'm going to let you practice," Lorna said.

I thought she would give me an orange. I'd heard of nursing students pricking needles into their peels to get the hang of it. Instead Lorna emptied one of the green tissue boxes that appeared everywhere at Sloan-Kettering to dry tears. Lorna turned the box upside down and poked in the type of needle contraption that would soon be stuck through Elliot's skin.

Lorna taped a bandage over the whole setup on the tissue box.

"Ok, first take off the tape, but be careful not to pull on the needle at the same time," she said. No problem. That was easy.

"Then hold the base down here, pull up on these wings and slide the needle into the safety catch," she said. I pulled. The needle slid right out. Fine. This didn't seem so bad.

It was time to try it for real. As I put on rubber gloves, tore open an antiseptic pad and got a pungent whiff of alcohol, my face flushed and my stomach tingled, like I was about to take an exam I didn't have enough time to study for. Think of all the little kids with Diabetes who managed their own insulin pricks, I told myself. Don't be a baby. Just do it. You took driving lessons in the white-knuckled chaos of the meat-packing district in Manhattan. You can do this too.

So I read my cheat sheet yet again, unscrewed a plastic connection on the IV tube, wiped it clean and flushed the port with saline to get it ready for my big maneuver. I took a deep breath.

Lorna watched as I pulled timidly at the edges of the bandage. Elliot winced as I ripped away patches of his chest chair. He refused to shave there despite several nurses' pleadings. His macho pride was at stake.

"It's okay," he said, grimacing. "Don't mind me. Keep going."

I held the base down and pulled the white wings together to slide them up the case. I tugged up gently. Hmmm. It wouldn't move. Hmmm. I tried again, a little harder. It wouldn't budge. Ok, harder still. Nope. Goddammit. This felt nothing like the tissue box. This thing just wouldn't give. I was terrified I'd rip the whole catheter through Elliot's skin in a bloody pulp. Or maybe I'd broken it.

"I can't do this," I blurted out in alarm. "I need help. I can't do this. It's stuck."

"You're fine, just pull," Lorna said.

"I can't, please. You have to. Please."

She slid it out in one deft sweep.

"No problem," she said. "You just need practice. You'll be fine next time."

"The box was so easy," I whimpered. "This felt nothing like the box."

"Don't worry about it," Elliot said as he leaned over to kiss my forehead. "You'll get the hang of it."

I stared at the grey linoleum floor, feeling like a failure. I could get into Yale but I couldn't yank out a stupid little needle? If Elliot could endure nausea, pain and despair about our lives forging on without him, I should be able to conquer this small task.

My next chance came two weeks later. This time I knew the needle would resist. I grit my teeth, squeezed my fingers on those exasperating white wings and pulled hard. In nothing short of a miracle, the wings rose. The needle was out. The whole contraption came away from his chest, free and clear. A tiny dot of blood showed where it had been. I covered it proudly with a Band-Aid.

"What a pro," Elliot said, beaming.

I think he liked having me fuss over him so tenderly, so eager to get it right and so afraid of hurting him. There was an intimacy there, a new mission and sense of purpose just between us. He watched me focus with an anxious brow on ministering to his body, only his, and a part of me was pleased to have him so dependent on me, only me. He couldn't even take a shower without my help. (I drew the line at giving him shots; he had to master blood-thinner injections himself.) Elliot appreciated everything I was trying to do. He told me all the time. Good thing, too. If he had taken my efforts for granted, I would have been stratospherically resentful.

I yanked off my rubber gloves with a flourish and threw them in the trash.

"Every time I do this I want you to bring me flowers," I announced. "That's the deal."

There were times over the next few months when we lay down to sleep and Elliot was connected to two long tubes, the chemo bottle and the bile bag. We didn't want them on the bed so we put them on Alex's red crate of Legos, which happened to be the right size to hold them at his side. We absorbed these unappetizing new attachments because we had no choice. We were just happy to be home together and developed enormous abilities to pretend they were not there. Sometimes blindness is a healthy choice.

And then, later in the spring, when that stupid bag was no longer needed, we had a little party for ourselves in bed. Elliot's body was whole again, at least on the outside, smooth and lean, muscled and unfettered. Its simple integrity was beautiful to behold. We felt so free. There was nothing that might get tangled up if we rolled around. After a stint tied to these medical devices, you can truly appreciate the miracle of being unencumbered, left alone together, to savor your own bare skins.

Leslie detaches a chemo IV from a port near Elliot's collarbone, summer 2007. Photo courtesy of *The Record*.

BELONGING

The University Club at Fifty-Fourth and Fifth is housed in one of the grandest architectural landmarks in Manhattan. Built in 1899 to look like an Italian Renaissance palazzo, its lobby has marble floors, imposing columns and lofty ceilings. There's always an extravagant bouquet of fresh flowers on a center table. The subdued tones of discreet conversation lend it the hushed, sober air of an aristocrat's library.

I had a love-hate relationship with the place.

Whenever I tiptoed into my father's exclusive club I regressed to feeling like a schoolgirl about to get in trouble with the principal. There were so many rules. No cell phones. No business meetings. No press interviews.

"Please be reminded that the Dress Code in the club is jacket and tie for gentlemen, similar formality for ladies," read the letter left on the pillow for guests who stayed overnight in its plush hotel rooms. The warning came with a blue velvet pouch holding a miniature chocolate square covered in gold foil and the UC insignia.

Logistically, it was a godsend. The University Club happened to be a few blocks away from the chemo clinic. After months of arranging my work schedule so I could drive Elliot back and forth to treatments, I was worn out and asked my parents if we could please stay overnight at the club sometimes beforehand. They generously agreed; it was one way they could help us from afar. They considered the club their home in the city. Especially for my mother, it was easier to give us access to the club than do something she found awkward, like asking me how Elliot was doing. An intensely private person, she seemed embarrassed by his medical problems or didn't want to intrude. Whatever the case, she rarely mentioned Elliot's illness or my efforts to take care of him.

While the club's convenience was a gift, I felt uncomfortable there. In recent years women had been allowed to join. Even so, as I read the long rows of hand-painted names of club officials and their alma maters on the wall by the elevator, I felt I didn't belong, even though I graduated from one of those hallowed schools, magna cum laude no less. Getting a name on that wall meant something else: business acumen, power, and kinship with the pinstriped masters of the universe.

I was a three-day-a-week reporter whose paycheck would get a laugh out of the concierge. This fancy club embodied the life I had once envisioned, perhaps married to a financial whiz, throwing chic dinner parties and summering in a second home in the Hamptons. As a teenager I thought my life would reflect the trendy pages of *New York Magazine.* Instead, my path had taken so many unexpected twists—a house in New Jersey, a C-section, divorce, step-kids, cancer, and a husband who hated to put on a suit. Half the times we went to that club I had to sneak Elliot up the back freight elevator so my dad wouldn't get demerits for our violations of the dress code. It stressed me to my very bones to think I might get my father disciplined because of Elliot's stubborn rebellious streak. Somehow this place hit the core of one of my deepest personal conflicts; the clash between my father's world view and my husband's.

One was politically conservative, the other argumentatively liberal. One respected financial achievement, the other—who edited endless stories about insider trading and white-collar crime—was suspicious of what it could take to get rich. One valued refinement, the other remained resolutely casual.

"I work like a dog all day and can barely buckle my belt sometimes from stomach cramps, for Chrissake," Elliot would grumble about dressing up for a night at the club. "Can't they give me a break about the damn jacket?"

"When in Rome, Sweetie," I'd say quietly. "If you want to stay here…"

The two most important men in my life never recognized how much they had in common. Both had modest roots in New York City. Both respected their Jewish heritage but didn't believe in God. I loved them both, both loved me, and each thought the other tried to control me too much.

My father, Gene Brody, took pride in this club, especially its library, the largest private book collection in the world. He had earned his way in. Growing up playing stickball in the streets of Brooklyn in the depths of the Depression, he was smart, ambitious and determined to carve his way in a wider, wealthier world. After graduating from Wharton and serving in the U. S. Navy, he went to night school at New York University to get an MBA. He had a keen talent for math and a fiercely independent mind, and the innovations in his graduate thesis on options won him a job on Wall Street. He worked hard and became quite a player in the 1960s. The boy who had watched his own father flounder through one unsuccessful business venture after another was proud to be wearing silk ties, playing squash at lunch and taking his young family skiing in France.

My tall, handsome father was widely respected for his integrity, warmth and humor. But this club he cherished smacked to me of a different sensibility. It felt judgmental and cold.

In time, however, Elliot and I became more comfortable there. We had to. The club's location simply made our lives so much easier.

I would drive into the city after work on Wednesdays with our suitcase and meet Elliot for our sacred date night. Often we'd indulge in the club's lavish seafood buffet. There was something surreal about what became a ritual: lobster the night before chemo, then pancakes for breakfast at Burger Heaven. After this priceless romantic interlude, it was time for a draining Thursday at the clinic, a few days of Elliot's groggy recuperation on the couch and then gearing back up for work on Monday.

For all his balking at the club's formality, Elliot appreciated the luxury and the privilege of spending time alone together. Our favorite room was 310. Its big, clean windows looked down on the glittering storefronts of Fifth Avenue.

As I walked through the club's lobby time after time, I looked for a way to make peace with my sense of self. One night I watched a well-coiffed woman with shiny patent pumps get irritated waiting for the elevator. So little patience. She may have been used to running the show in the club's universe, but I wondered how well she would manage what I was doing—unhooking IVs, washing sheets drenched with night sweats and taking care of children who were putting up with an awful lot of drama. Maybe she wouldn't succeed in my world.

WAITING
April 2007

It was spring, time for another CT scan. Elliot had one about every two months to see whether the drugs were working. There was an emotional pattern that went along with these tests: a buildup of anxiety beforehand, impatience while waiting a few days for results, then a rush of relief or crushing disappointment.

As Elliot was undergoing the scan, I sat on a nubby beige couch in a waiting room, yet again, for hours, and scribbled down my thoughts. If I put them on paper they would stop swirling around in my brain, harassing me. I didn't have anything to write on but a printout of a recipe for pork ribs that a friend had sent in an email. That had to suffice.

"E is in CT scan," I wrote. "I'm reading *The New Yorker* review of Joan Didion's play *The Year of Magical Thinking*. I'm morbidly drawn to these reviews, like she could give me a hint of what's to come, as though if I suffer now in anticipation I'll be inoculated, better prepared when it really happens.

"The reviewer quotes Didion: 'We all know that if we are to live ourselves there comes a time when we must relinquish the dead…I knew that as the second year began and the days passed…my sense of John and Quintana alive would become more remote, softened, transmuted into whatever best served my life without them.'

"It would be so sad to feel my life with E had become remote. I remember when I was a teenager and our dog Daisy died, how quickly it felt like normal to be without her and how far away our time with her seemed to be. To let his presence fade so fast would be an insult to our marriage. It's morose to be contemplating what it will feel like when he dies.

"On the way down here I thought about how I define myself so much now as a wife and nurse, and don't feel as accomplished as a reporter. So it will feel so empty to be just a reporter again. Yes, I'm a mother too, and I love that, and think I'm good at it, but that feels like a necessary minimum requirement. I guess I'll have to invest more in being a friend. Maybe I'll try writing a book, even if it doesn't get read or published, even if Calvin Trillin and Joan Didion—far better writers, of course—have written all this before, and surely with more precision and insight. It doesn't hurt to try."

I felt stuck in such a strange limbo. Growing up I had always been in a rush—to get good grades, a job, a family of my own. But this was a time when I could not do what it would take to prepare for the next stage, a future when I would probably need a new job to make more money to support my kids. I would have to recreate a whole new life someday, but it was impossible to start lining up the building blocks, redoing the resume, sending out applications, taking the early-bird steps that made a goodie-goodie feel like she was being responsible, doing her homework in advance. I didn't know when this new future would start, and didn't want to look to Elliot like I was clearing the path for a life without him. Yet I was not used to procrastinating. Putting everything on hold was an uncomfortable discipline to master.

He's here now, I told myself. Just be with him.

A chatterbox sitting nearby interrupted my scribbling. She said she'd been going through treatment for sixteen years.

"When my mom and dad made me they put in some cement," she said with a laugh.

Sixteen years of this limbo? I couldn't imagine it. But the alternative was so much worse.

Don't think so much about the future, I told myself.

Don't be afraid to grow closer.

Don't mourn his death before it happens.

You'll have plenty of time for that later. Plenty.

Elliot wasn't giving up on the possibility of many good days ahead. He had just seen me trying out Crest Whitestrips to bleach my teeth and decided to try it too. A funny joint project. Intimate, I guess. I was glad he was doing something for the future, not presuming it wouldn't matter anymore. Maybe the anti-anxiety drugs mellowed him out and lulled him into denial. Maybe I could have used some of those pacifiers myself, but there was too much pressure on me to be alert, make decisions, react to symptoms, plan for contingencies. I was the one who had to drive. I couldn't afford to be woozy from Ativan.

"It bothers me that I'm not spending my time sitting here wishing for a good result on this CT scan," I wrote. "I assume all this will end badly at some point. Maybe a tiny part of me just wants the whole ordeal over with. But then what will I be?

"Just wishing to be back here, waiting."

Exhaustion makes everything more depressing. It was a beautiful spring morning, but I didn't feel the sense of renewal that comes when the air gets warmer and the purple crocuses pop up. Each day that passed brought us closer to that vague deadline, so haunting and mysterious. "Lucky to live a year or two," the doctors had said. Is it better to be given a time frame like that, or is it better to have no clue?

Time is a precious commodity. I didn't want to waste it in wallowing. But I couldn't escape the sense we were losing it fast, that we were nearing the halfway mark of this journey, that soon we would have less time ahead of us than we had already spent since Elliot's diagnosis. I felt utterly powerless.

Sometimes I saw myself like a car in a car wash, stuck on a conveyor belt, being moved inexorably forward without any control. The car gets smacked in the face by hoses, then soap, then scrubbers and brushes, then more hoses. The windshield takes one hit after another. The car has to just put up with whatever comes, and in the end rolls out looking shiny and fresh. But I was feeling more and more bedraggled.

My favorite cancer patient wasn't losing his hair, but I was, from the sheer stress of it all.

WHAT ABOUT THE REST OF US?
April 2007

When we schlepped to the city yet again for Elliot's umpteenth round of chemo and the results of his latest CT scan, we got good news for a change. The second set of drugs seemed to have gotten the tumors under control. This was something to celebrate. We had a fight instead.

Our bickering started after I checked the clinic's public computer in the fourth floor waiting room. There was an email from Alex's baseball coach announcing an 8:00 a.m. practice the next day when school would be closed for Good Friday.

"That's ridiculous," Elliot snapped when I told him. "Practice on a holiday? That's so intrusive. If you have to take Alex to baseball how can we have breakfast together?"

"It's not such a big deal," I said. "You don't have to go anywhere. I'll just drop him off and come back."

"These Montclair parents have no boundaries," he said as we walked down the hallway toward the infusion unit. "They compete to do more and more and more for their kids' relentless activities and never leave any free time to relax or go to a museum, or God forbid spend any time as grownups."

My jaw clenched. The unit smelled like an odd mix of an old lady's perfume, someone's leftover tuna fish sandwich and the ammonia used to sterilize the floors. A receptionist ushered us into a small room with two big olive green BarcaLoungers for patients. Elliot groaned when he saw this room had no windows. He always insisted that a chair with a view was essential to his sanity. A heavy-set, weary-looking guy in there already was hooked up to an IV, trying to doze.

My stomach was knotted with tension, as if a spool of wire in my gut were getting pulled tighter and tighter. What days I worked, what we ate, when we ate, when we went to bed, where we could go on vacation, everything was defined by Elliot's medical needs. I couldn't stand to hear him complain about one of the few things that revolved around my son. An energetic ten-year-old, Alex was on two baseball teams. He adored the sport, wanted to get better, and had to play on the second spring team if he wanted a spot in the summer league.

"Being on two teams is too much," Elliot insisted as he rolled up a sleeve to get ready for the nurse. "It's taking over our life. Devon's got her riding on Sundays so the whole weekend's booked before it even starts. I drag my sorry ass into the city every day for work or doctors' appointments. After all that I deserve some freedom on the weekends."

"We hardly see all of Alex's games," I said.

The poor guy in the chair next to us was pretending to be asleep. These quarters were way too close for such a personal dispute, but I was tired of always being the accommodator, smoothing over every bump.

I wished we had a laptop. At home we argued by email, even when we were in the same room, because I never wanted the kids to hear us fight. A verbal fire hose, Elliot would start pouring out his legal brief and I couldn't get in a word, so I'd sit at the computer and pound out a response. Then he'd say "my turn," push his way into the computer chair and bang out a reply. We'd carry on like this, taking turns at the keyboard, until we petered out. Sometimes we simmered overnight, but by lunch the next day, it would be over.

"Truce," one of us would email.

"Okay," the other would answer.

Inside the clinic we did not have the benefit of such high-tech mediation.

"You write all these stories about overscheduled kids and then you go and overschedule yours," Elliot argued.

"Chemo can't be the main thing on the calendar!" I spat back.

Elliot was the one who taught Alex the joy of baseball. It had become their deepest bond. So now, after Elliot created this little baseball nut, he was trying to limit his ability to participate? I didn't relish the idea of driving Alex back and forth to an 8:00 a.m. practice either, but it wasn't that big a deal. What I really wanted to do was skip our usual long lazy vacation day breakfast and go to the gym. Between work, chemo, all the household chores and the kids, I never got any exercise anymore. My big indulgence was a once-a-month book club meeting, and sometimes Elliot gave me a sad puppy face when I gathered up my keys for that. As much as I loved feeling so important to him, his dependency could be imprisoning. He had always been clingy, but this illness had intensified his neediness and even made it legitimate.

My mother bear claws were getting ready to strike, just as they did whenever I felt my kids' best interests under attack. Devon and Alex deserved to have passions outside the house and needed their healthy distractions, especially with all this cancer business going on. They would be little only once. I couldn't put their lives on hold until Elliot's situation "got resolved." That was my euphemism, at least in public or with the kids. Got resolved.

This whole conflict hurt so much because I longed for my kids to love Elliot. I didn't want them to think of him as the killjoy who came into our lives and said no to the fun things they cared about. What if they secretly wished him gone so they could do as they pleased and have me all to themselves? Then they would be consumed by guilt when he died, as if their wishes had made it happen. I could understand the desire for such freedom. There were times when I thought about how much easier my life would be when all this was over. So much sadder, but easier.

I was fuming silently about all this when a trim, pretty blond nurse with a peppy ponytail pulled aside the cubicle's sliding door and started to go through Elliot's chart.

"How are we today?" she chirped.

You don't want to know, I thought to myself. Elliot was trying to relax in his big soft BarcaLounger. I was balancing on the little hardwood chair squeezed in there for the patient's hand-holder. The cubicle was so cramped I had our jackets and his knapsack in my lap. I stewed about this too. The clinic's brochures all talked about how the caregiver needs support, but my chair was too rigid, upright and angular to be comfortable. While Elliot could nap for the hour or two of this infusion, I had to keep shifting positions. I couldn't help resenting the fact that nobody cared if I got any rest. I was the one who would drive us back through rush hour, who would have to make dinner while Elliot was sleeping, who had to make sure the kids got their tests signed and dentist appointments booked and presents ready for the next bar mitzvahs. These chemo trips ate up the whole day, what with waiting for the blood test results, the doctor, the drugs to be mixed and an infusion room to open up. And it was like that every two weeks. Of course it could be much worse. Elliot could be even sicker. Or he could be a child. But for the moment I wanted to flip the finger at such perspective and rage.

"So Mr. Pinsley, do you have any nausea or diarrhea?" the petite nurse asked as she filled out the routine questionnaire on symptoms. "Any tingling? Numbness? Mouth sores?"

"What about irritability," I burst out. "Why don't you ever ask about that?"

The nurse was taken aback. I didn't care.

"And why don't you ever ask how I am? Why is everything always about the patient? What about the exhausted family who has to take care of him?"

Somebody else's IV monitor beeped with urgency.

"I'll be right back," the nurse said as she scurried away, surely glad for a reason to flee. Elliot and I sat in tight-lipped silence.

The nurse returned a few minutes later to jab a needle into the port in his chest and get his IV started. She must have thought me such a shrew, giving my husband a hard time while poison pumped into his veins. My cheeks burned with anger and shame and disgust at my lost temper, but it's impossible to go through so much stress, for so long, without ever fighting. Still I was haunted by the possibility of infinite regrets if something horrible should happen that very night. Would I want these to be our final hours together? That question, always present, put an awful lot of pressure on every single encounter.

What I was discovering, alas, was the strain of living each day as if it could be Elliot's last. It puts a mountain of stress on a marriage, and a family, when one person's needs are so intense and undeniable. There's no balance to the negotiations that are an integral part of resolving the competing demands of normal, everyday life.

Elliot needed me. He needed me to drive him home, to make his food, to get his medicine from the drug store. He would need me in two days to unhook his IV. We would have to make up soon enough. This was too hard a road to travel without getting mad at each other sometimes, but it was even harder to go it alone.

And so, as I drove my drowsy husband back over the George Washington Bridge, I gave in, took the fall, apologized. I just couldn't bear to let the quarrel drag out.

"I'm sorry, we're both just too tired," I said. He nodded, put his hand on my knee and closed his eyes to doze.

And the next morning I took Alex to baseball.

It wasn't the last time this issue flared up. Any conflicts between us usually centered on who came first, my husband or my kids. I was stuck in the middle, torn between them, and I got tired of being the diplomat. Maybe if we'd been together longer we would have worked all this out already. We'd been married only six years when Elliot got sick. I read once it takes seven years for a stepfamily to feel like a unit. In some ways, his illness became a crucible. It amplified his needs and forced me to stand up for my kids when they deserved my time and attention. Maybe that's the key to a good marriage—emerging from negotiations with respect instead of resentment. Maybe a marriage is like a muscle that you have to strain and flex and stretch to strengthen. If you just let it lie there, comfortable, it becomes lax and weak.

"Listen, first off, I love you and I love the kids," Elliot wrote me after a similar dust-up. "One way or another, for all my occasional gruffness, I think you all know that. Or should. Second, among the unspoken issues in our life is the irrefutable reality that so many of the family-life/balance issues are things I went through with my three kids before. It doesn't make me an expert, but it does make me a tad wearier, going through it again now, at fifty-six, with Devon and Alex, no less as I'm battling cancer and daily fatigue. That doesn't mean they should be deprived of things that make them happy, things they like to do and should do. But maybe it should mean that you need to understand that my capacity to adjust to their often over-busy schedules and the concomitant late dinners, rushed breakfasts and the general sense that our life is a whirlwind of kid activities, is somewhat diminished…. I'm doing my best to accommodate, but frankly, I need things to be a little less scheduled and hectic, a little easier."

"Okay," I wrote back. "Truce."

Time and again I gave in, probably more easily than I should have. But the guy with the cancer always had the trump card. Barring another unexpected catastrophe, my children and I were going to be together for a long time, longer than Elliot would be with us. I hated thinking about that, but it was the bitter truth. There would come a day, unfortunately, when I could do with my children whatever I wanted. For the time being, while Elliot was with us, I would make sure they had what they needed, but real balance would come only over the long haul. I could only hope that my children would learn to emulate my empathy rather than my tendency to submit.

94

WHY I BEGAN TO WRITE
May 2007

Back in late August, soon after Elliot's diagnosis, a legendary reporter named Tom Hallman Jr. came to *The Record*. He'd written *The Boy Behind the Mask*, a Pulitzer Prize-winning series in *The Oregonian* about a child who had grown up with horrific facial disfigurement from a life-threatening disease. After years of pitying stares and loneliness, the boy went through a gauntlet of difficult surgeries and finally fought his way back from a coma. It is a miraculous story. Hallman came to talk to the newsroom about the power of narrative non-fiction.

"Write about what means the most to you," Hallman told us. "If it matters to you it will resonate with readers."

What mattered most to me was my husband's death sentence, but I was reluctant to write about that. I didn't want to sound whiny, exhibitionistic or attention-seeking. I didn't want to seem like I was exploiting a family tragedy to advance my career. And I wasn't sure how I could write honestly about Elliot's illness without spilling more details about his prognosis than I wanted our children to know.

During the lunch break I sat down next to Hallman in the noisy office cafeteria. My mouth was so dry I could barely swallow my ham sandwich. After we chatted for a while I screwed up the courage to tell him what I was considering. After saying he was sorry to hear my news, he encouraged me to write about it.

"I'm always drawn to stories about choice," he said.

"Choice?" I asked, confused. "What choice?"

"You can join your husband on this emotional journey or you can back away," he said.

The voice of that very first social worker echoed in my head, saying "Don't be afraid to get closer." That had sounded so daunting at first, and certain to cause me even more heartache when I finally lost the man who made me so happy, but I had come to think of it as the only option. "Backing away" was tantamount to abandonment.

"I'm just not sure it's a good idea to expose my family," I told Hallman.

When I got home that night, still toying with the notion of proposing a newspaper series on our ordeal, I was disgusted to find myself listening to Elliot in a different way—with an ear searching for workable quotes instead of real connection. I decided right then to ditch the whole idea. I had long been in the habit of saving sweet mementos—even writing down amusing conversations—but taking notes on my husband, observing him for details that would catch a reader's attention, seemed like a very different project and I was afraid it would come between us. I would be treating Elliot like an object of scrutiny instead of a partner. I felt my cheeks flush hot, as if I'd been tempted to sell my marriage for the sake of a better resume.

A few days later I got a kind email from Hallman.

"Even if you don't ever write about this, keep a journal," he suggested. "One day you may find a reason to write this story."

He was right. Nine months later, the friend who sat next to me at work got her own wallop of terrible news. She had breast cancer. Lindy Washburn is one of the most talented reporters I know. I had spent years applauding as prestigious national awards streamed in for her ambitious, hard-hitting articles on health care. Naturally, soon after she was diagnosed, she told me she wanted to write a series based on her cancer experience.

I watched as she threaded her way between the grey, messy cubicles to get to the top editor's glass-walled office. I could see her neat blond head nodding as they discussed it. That got my competitive juices flowing. I sat at my desk feeling dizzy with adrenaline. A freezing tremble took over, the kind I get when I'm really nervous.

What bothered me was more than envy that Lindy had the balls to go after what I had talked myself out of attempting. I just couldn't bear to sit there yet again, just a few feet away from her desk, hearing the inevitable accolades and sympathy and marveling over the patient's side of the story.

"This is hard for me too!" I wanted to scream. "I know the patient has to go through hideous pain and nausea and fear. But I'm going to be left alone! Devastated! When Elliot's trial is over, I'm the one who's going to have to pick up all the pieces and take care of everybody in their anguish. What about me?"

On top of all that--and with my deepest apologies to Lindy and anyone else who has fought this particular devil-I was so damn sick of hearing about breast cancer. Of course it could be terrifying and excruciating and I knew wonderful women who had died from it. But I envied that most of them had the potential, at least, for optimism. Breast cancer had an eighty-eight percent survival rate five years past diagnosis! Pancreatic cancer's survival rate was six percent. It's unseemly to compare cancers like they're in some kind of competition—and no doubt advocates for diabetes and brain injuries and other killers are jealous of cancer's domination in the media. Still, I was so tired of pink ribbons and pink cupcakes and breast cancer awareness campaigns. Everybody was aware of breast cancer. Pancreatic cancer was the fourth leading cause of cancer death but got only two percent of the National Cancer Institute's funding for research because it didn't have sexy crusaders like Sheryl Crowe or Christina Applegate who lived long enough to fight for it. It didn't have the primal mommy factor. It wasn't about tits.

That's not exactly what I said when I banged out an email to the top editor. "I'd like to propose a set of complementary stories from the caregiver's perspective," I wrote. "It's a tough battle of a different kind and it's a relatively untold story that affects a huge swath of our readers."

The editor agreed on the spot. Lindy and I would write our stories separately but use the same "Living with Cancer" logo.

Elliot was a sport, encouraging me as always.

"Just take out all those adjectives in front of my name," he said as he looked over a draft sprinkled with adoring modifiers like smart and handsome and brave. "I find them personally embarrassing."

I wrote my heart out in those stories, and the truth is that I didn't do it primarily for readers' edification. I did it for my own selfish reasons because I was angry and resentful and an approval junkie. I loved my husband desperately, but if I was going to spend countless hours in hospitals, miss many of my son's baseball games, endure post-chemo crankiness, do all the chores at home and put my life on hold to give Elliot the best possible final days, I wanted to be appreciated for it. He was deeply grateful, and showed it, and that was a beautiful thing, but I was insatiable for appreciation on some kind of cosmic level. Writing that series was like venting to a half-million readers. It was like yelling to the universe, CAN YOU BELIEVE THIS IS HAPPENING? To us? To me?

I smiled and acted stoic on the outside. On the inside I felt ripped off and wrung out. But the person who is not sick is not supposed to complain. This series was my rant, journalism as self-expression. It was fueled, I suppose, by the same furious impulse that drives so many patients and families to blog. For some people, including me, it was impossible to keep these exasperations quiet.

That series, which ended up with about twenty articles in all, had some unexpected results.

It resonated with readers far more than I imagined. I got a flood of letters and emails from husbands and wives and grown children with caregiving burdens who said the stories made them feel less alone. I found myself instantly connected to a community of people who understood what I was going through. It was deeply satisfying to see that my stories and Lindy's did do some good. They steered people to support groups, inspired the launch of local lecture programs, raised money for research, explained the pros and cons of joining clinical trials and urged doctors to be more sensitive about delivering awful news.

My favorite letter came from a man who said the stories helped him appreciate his wife. "My dear Marianne got me through two bouts of cancer and I never realized how hard it was for her to keep my spirits up until I read your article," he wrote in spindly script. "Thank you."

The biggest surprise came from Max, who was with us during a break from college in Ithaca. I didn't think he'd read any of the series but he mentioned one installment on how the caregiver's need for support is often overlooked.

"It was good," he said.

"I'm glad to hear you say that," I said. "I was afraid you might not like it."

"Why? You're the one doing all the work. We appreciate it."

Max mentioned the stories to Elliot as well, saying he didn't realize the medical stuff had gotten so intense at home while he was away at college.

"I feel bad about it because I only see you on holidays and weekends," he said with apologetic concern.

"He's turning into a real mensch," Elliot told me with pride.

That was something I never dreamed of. That my family would end up communicating more about the most significant issue in our lives because we could read about it in the pages of *The Record*.

There was another benefit I hadn't figured on. Since I wanted more voices from people going through this nightmare, I decided to try a support group. I never would have gone without a professional research purpose egging me on. I was afraid of being brought down by other people's troubles at a time when I was trying so hard not to sink from the weight of our own. But the possibility I might find some fellow husbands and wives to interview gave me an incentive.

The caregiver support group met on Tuesday nights a few blocks from my office at the Hackensack branch of Gilda's Club, the social refuge for people affected by cancer. The international organization was launched by Gene Wilder, the widower of the *Saturday Night Live* comedienne Gilda Radner, who died of ovarian cancer and said laughter was the best tool for coping.

I was nervous the first time I walked though those signature red doors on a warm summer evening about a year after Elliot's diagnosis. I didn't feel like a self-help type and was afraid these overwhelmed souls would disdain me as a media spy taking advantage of my access. Elliot would never join such a group. He divided cancer patients into two camps; those who wanted to learn as much as they could about their disease and talk about it, and those who would rather do just about anything else. He had clearly dug in among the latter.

A trained facilitator opened the Gilda's Club meeting by introducing me. Ten men and women sat in a circle in a small lounge lined with plush couches upholstered with cheery pink, green and beige floral patterns. Most were older than I was, retired and clinging to this group like a lifeline. They looked kindly, sad-eyed and depleted.

"Hi, my name is Leslie," I said. "I just want you to know that I'm here as a wife and as a reporter. I'm writing about taking care of my husband for *The Record* but I promise I won't use anything you say here unless I get your explicit permission. I hope that's okay."

They nodded and smiled, glad the paper was acknowledging that their experience was an important subject. A few had read my stories.

That group was nothing like what I expected.

For one thing, these people were incredibly funny. Gallows humor, for sure. They took enormous satisfaction in having someplace to express aggravations they felt wouldn't be understood "out there." They regaled the room with stories, sometimes sidesplitting, sometimes heartbreaking, about sick spouses who were unbearably irritable, selfish relatives who promised to help but didn't come through, and longtime friends who dropped them like lepers when cancer cropped up.

It was astonishing to discover the comforting power in a circle of people who fully understood what you were going through because they'd been there too. It certainly helped that these were wise, droll people from interesting backgrounds—a commercial artist, an inner-city teacher and a manager of public opinion polls for New York newsrooms. They were not the types to indulge in self-pity. They came for a break, strategic advice and compassion. Several quoted the proverb about the man who cursed that he had no shoes until he saw a man who had no feet. (For me, that man was a little boy who beamed as he showed off that if he stood on his tippy toes he could push the elevator button at Sloan-Kettering. He had a chemo pump like Elliot's tucked in his Mickey Mouse backpack.)

These husbands and wives were devoted but on the brink. Two women had been tempted to flee. One said her husband became so depressed and abusive during years of treatment that her children encouraged her to get a divorce. She toughed it out instead. The other had to quit her job to take care of her husband, who had one horrible complication after another for six years. Then he developed a severe case of "chemo brain," a version of memory loss that might be a side effect of some drugs. Her husband constantly asked her the same questions, over and over.

"At times, I've told him I'm running away, I can't bear it any longer," she admitted. "But I could never do that, as much as I fantasize about it. We've been together thirty-five years, and I love him dearly."

She brought me back to the words of Tom Hallman, the writer. "You can join your husband on this emotional journey or you can back away…"

The support group meetings always contained a few eye-poppers. One man told of an impossible neighbor who kept bugging him about cutting the lawn.

"Does the guy know your wife's in the hospital?" another man asked.

"Yes, but he doesn't care."

"Well then tell him he can wipe my ass."

"Been there," said one woman wryly.

"Done that," another chimed in.

Oh Jesus, I thought. These women had to do to *that* for their husbands? Please let us be spared that indignity. Please. The other women were chuckling. They had gotten used to such things. I was a rookie. I was horrified.

Despite those ominous allusions, I left those meetings feeling a little lighter. After a few months, though, I dropped out because my favorite participants either moved away, or, sadly, moved on to the bereavement group. Plus, I hated being away from my kids an extra night before chemo trips. Out of tens of thousands of cancer caregivers in northern New Jersey, only a handful attended these support groups, so I wasn't the only one who felt conflicted.

Still, the ten veterans in that little room blessed me with better perspective; for everything Elliot and I had gone through, we were having a relatively smooth ride. And we had each other. On good days we were still playing our sloppy but earnest games of tennis, biking around town and holding hands on the tabletop at dinner. It could be a helluva lot worse.

He was being a gladiator. So was I. Hearing how badly some patients treated their spouses— intentionally or not—made me appreciate Elliot's tenderness all the more, and made me feel even more bound to him with a shared sense of purpose. We wanted to squeeze the most we could out of our time together and help our children feel as close, loved and strong as possible. Our days were complicated but our mission was clear.

WISPS OF WORRY
Summer 2007

I tried to protect my kids during this time and keep a close eye on their moods. If all this illness was getting to be too rough on them, I wanted to know.

Once I found a clue in the garbage. I noticed my daughter, on a rare spree to clean up her room after the end of seventh grade, had jumped to throw out a short story she'd written for English. She seemed to be hiding something, so I dug the crumpled paper out of the trash, rationalizing that anything was fair in the effort to discern whether she was in some kind of distress. The story was about "the sandwich guy" in the school cafeteria and how he understood her. I read it with trepidation.

"Maybe he sees me, for just half a second, sitting at my lunch table, and he notices something is bothering me, and no one around me really knows what it is…Maybe he knows that I wish this summer we could go to the Grand Canyon so that when this ends my stepdad, Joe, would have gone there. Maybe he knows why I sit through endless baseball games and just listen to Joe breathing next to me so in ten years I can remember. Maybe he knows why I'll go sit with the guy when it's just us in the house, just sit with him in the room and make sure he's still there and won't fade away like in the movies, and I can just hold on to his hair (which I hope doesn't start to fall out soon because that's what happens in the books, but please I hope it doesn't because then I would just cry) and know that yes, he's still here, even though he has a pump in his side, and we have to sit at dinner and wait for him while our food is getting cold so he can give himself shot after shot so that maybe he'll get better."

I had no idea Devon was trying to savor simple moments with her stepfather, and memorize him, just like me.

The next section about the "sandwich guy" recapped the night we were having dinner with Elliot's mother, and somehow the subject of genetic counseling came up. I started jotting down some notes on Elliot's relatives but Devon thought my handwriting was atrocious and grabbed the pen out of my hand to do it herself.

"Maybe he knows that I had to make a family tree (for the doctors) of every person in my stepdad's family who had died of it, that I had to put how old they were and what type of cancer and when they died, and next to his name was just a blank, gaping hole just waiting to be filled, just staring at me like a kid with wide, expectant eyes who wants to know the answer, and I would yell 'I don't know!!! How should I know???' But the 'kid' doesn't look away, because really, I am the kid, and the question tinges all my thoughts like the brown on the roast beef, and it doesn't go away."

Damn. I had wondered if that genealogy conversation had been too morbid, but it got going before I could cut it off, and then Devon seemed to want to take charge of the family tree, and I thought maybe it would make her feel good to help. Hushing up the conversation might have been worse, might have suggested things were so dire that we couldn't even discuss them. Who knows? How can a parent prepare for on-the-spot dilemmas like this?

On the outside the kids seemed fine. They went about their business, did their homework, saw friends and unloaded the dishwasher when prodded. Jonathan Alter, a *Newsweek* columnist who had lymphoma, wrote that his kids were protected by the "glorious narcissism of adolescence," and I'd assumed my kids were a bit sheltered that way too. (Devon would later disabuse me of that notion. In her view, Alter was dead wrong. "Kids are a lot more aware than they're given credit for," she said. "People always underestimate them. It's obvious what's going on.")

They were watching Elliot closely. They had come to depend on him. When Alex was little he used to dress up in costumes to meet Elliot at the train. He'd be Spiderman, Homer Simpson, a businessman or a clown. The kids loved how Elliot brought them Krispy Kreme donuts for good report cards and the way he moaned in mock exasperation at my chronically silly puns ("Look, there's picture of a newt in the paper. It's a newts-paper! You don't like my puns? So give me pun-icillin!") They knew he made me happy, and they were worried.

I did some more research into how to talk to children about cancer as the disease progressed. The experts said you should use simple, straightforward language. Kids need repeated reassurance that their needs will be met, they can't catch cancer like a cold, and it's not their fault. Even some teenagers blame themselves, assuming their yelling or rebellious behavior drove their parents to collapse.

Children have such keen antennae, experts advised against keeping secrets. Considering all the meds and symptoms and ER visits, I can't even imagine how that would be logistically possible, but I'd met some parents who tried, like an Orthodox Jewish couple with five young children. Stage IV breast cancer had kept the mom in bed countless days over a year and a half, but she simply said "Mommy has a boo-boo" and God would take care of her.

Most experts agree that kids who aren't told what's going on can feel betrayed when the truth eventually comes out. One social worker told me that parents who think their children aren't aware of a cancer diagnosis in the family should check what they've Googled lately. "Sure enough they find 'leukemia'," she said. "They are so surprised."

Some kids feel guilty for resenting a sick relative. Some feel selfish if they have fun with friends during a crisis. Some get depressed watching a parent get weak. Private counseling and support groups give children a safe place to unburden themselves, but my kids wanted none of that.

Many children try to hide their fears from their families because they don't want to add another burden to the pile. I guess that's why Devon threw her short story in the trash.

She tried to keep a poem from me too. Her class had been studying Greek odes and she had to devise one of her own. I opened the school literary magazine one spring day and there it was.

ODE TO MY MOTHER'S HAIRBAND

Thank you, my strand of connection
The only thing holding
Chaos together.
Wisps of worry frame her face…
And I see her
About to fall off
But at least you hold some of her together
Keep some strings attached
So we can have her presence
Even if not whole.
Perhaps you are all-knowing
Wise enough
To bend and snap on others
But be gentle on her.
But please
Don't betray
And break
We all need to pretend
To have some
Control.

What to say about such a poem? Devon saw us teetering on the edge of chaos? She saw "wisps of worry" around my face? I was moved by her empathy ("be gentle on her") and admired her powers of observation, but I was upset to see she thought our family seemed about to fall apart. I was trying so hard to make our home feel warm and stable and safe.

She wanted my "presence even if not whole." She must have noticed how much of my attention was devoted to Elliot, but didn't sound bitter about it. That was a comfort.

I tried to talk to Devon about the poem. No go.

"Oh Mom," she groaned, rolling her eyes. "You weren't supposed to see that. I didn't give them permission to publish it."

Alex was a little more forthcoming. His questions about Elliot's cancer practically followed the script from the cancer books.

One night when I was stirring spaghetti sauce for dinner, about six months after Elliot got sick, Alex brought up the subject. We'd talked about a few of these issues before, but he seemed to want reassurance.

"Does Elliot have a mild kind of cancer or a serious one?" Alex asked.

"It's a tough one, but he's strong and determined and has very good doctors."

"Is it like the kind of cancer in the lung cancer commercial that can kill you?"

"It can, but I certainly hope it won't."

"How do you get it?"

We're not really sure, I explained, but sometimes it can be inherited, like blond hair.

"Can I get it then?"

"Well, we're a family but you and Elliot aren't related by blood."

"So it's not contagious?"

"No."

It wasn't easy to stay composed during conversations like this. Luckily, Alex's next question, "Where is a pancreas, anyway?" led us to an anatomy book where far more interesting body parts brought some comic relief.

I was glad to know he felt comfortable asking these questions. He ended up writing about Elliot's illness too.

"I think my family's life would be much easier if this never happened," Alex wrote in a fifth-grade essay. "He's in a bad mood lots of times because of chemotherapy, so after chemo it's really stressful."

That's for sure.

I didn't talk that much about the whole cancer business with Max, who was busy in college, and Aaron, working in Chicago. They didn't see the day-to-day ups and downs that my kids did. Kate, working in New York, had a clearer view because she came over a lot to have dinner or watch a ball game. She understood that visiting was the best medicine she could give.

All the kids wanted to do the right thing, and we didn't have to prod one bit to get them all to join us for a weeklong vacation in the Outer Banks. Aaron had never come on a summer trip with us before. Elliot looked so happy strolling along the ocean beach, seeing his whole group together. His kids saw the bump of his port under his collarbone for the first time. Aaron called him "Cyborg" after a comic book hero who had superhuman strength thanks to his mechanical implants.

"If something happens to Elliot, will we still see the Pinsleys?" Devon asked me one day.

"I certainly hope so," I replied. "They're our family."

DUMB THINGS PEOPLE SAY

Before I rail against the people who said truly bone-headed things about Elliot's illness, let me stop to thank the friends and neighbors who did everything right.

The good guys came out in remarkable force, bearing books, DVDs for diversion in the chemo clinic and even keys to a country house in Rhode Island (not to mention the stealthy deliveries of weed). Our friend Pam would sometimes show up at our door at 9:00 p.m. with a hot apple cobbler right out of the oven. Neighbors we didn't know very well kept coming by with homemade lasagna and roast chicken. My book club gave me gift cards for massages. Colleagues at work devised a weekly rotation to bring us dinners. That lasted almost six months, until Elliot was told to avoid fat and could no longer dig into their rich casseroles and cream pies. Alex was sorry to see the chocolate ones go.

Such warmth was stunning—especially to someone who grew up in New York apartment buildings where neighbors rarely knew each others' names. It was an enormous source of comfort to see how many truly caring people wanted to help us. It gave me deeper respect for the best of humankind.

At the same time, however, there were a few incidents of such crude insensitivity they made my jaw drop. It's understandable that people often don't know what to say or feel awkward in the company of someone with a serious illness, and I cringe to think of all the times I've blurted out something dumb. Some of the comments we heard, however, were hurtful and quite avoidable. I was trying hard to be careful about everyone's feelings inside my house and I didn't want some outsider mucking everything up.

Once at a school event a fellow parent came up to me and demanded, "So, how bad is it?" This man was a surgeon. He seemed to want to show that he was in the know, a master of the gory details. I hoped he left such cavalier pessimism behind when he talked to his own patients.

Another time, a long-lost friend of Elliot's swooped in out of the blue like a vulture, drawn to the juicy drama. After a few minutes on the phone catching up, my husband asked how he was doing.

"Well, at least I've got my health," the guy said with a dark laugh. Very funny.

Please don't get me wrong—reconnecting with old friends with sincere good will was one of the few benefits of this ordeal. It was the callers motivated by lurid curiosity who were galling. Carole Radziwill, in her memoir about her husband's illness, called them "tragedy whores."

Here's another favorite from a Christmas party. I had vowed to take a break from the medical mess. Knowing some people would ask how Elliot was doing, I had my line ready: "We're hanging in there, thanks for asking, and we're taking a vacation from the subject tonight." Period. Polite and firm.

Usually that worked. One nervy woman, however, refused to take the hint.

"Okay," she whispered to me conspiratorially. "But what's the one-sentence bottom line?"

What, you want a D-date? She never cared much about us when everyone was fine. Guess the gossip potential was irresistible.

One night Elliot and I bumped into a neighbor when both our families were picking out Christmas trees. It was supposed to be a Kodak moment.

"Hey, did you hear about Rob's father?" the neighbor said, alluding to another man on our block. "He had pancreatic cancer and lasted only two months so you're ahead of the game!"

Seriously? I didn't want to blow up in front of all the kids so I simply said Merry Christmas and walked away. But a few minutes later, when I saw the guy pull into his driveway, I marched up to his car.

"Can I talk to you a second please?" I asked, grabbing his arm to drag him out to the street so his little girls couldn't hear me sputter. "How could you possibly think that was a helpful thing to say?"

"I'm sorry," he said looking sheepishly at the pavement. "I'm famous for putting my feet in my mouth."

"Yeah, well, be more careful."

He was so embarrassed afterwards that he avoided Elliot altogether. The two of them used to share their train commute to the city and chat daily on the platform. The man simply disappeared from the 8:57.

I got so fed up with these ugly incidents I wrote an essay for *The Record* about what not to say, and what to do, when a family you care about faces a severe illness. It must have hit a nerve; it drew emails from as far as Israel. One reader, Cynthia, wrote me about the hellish days when her seven-year-old daughter was dying. Her husband vowed to open a guard booth in the lobby of Sloan-Kettering. He would bar entry to anyone who said "you can always have more children" or "when God closes a door, he opens a window."

Here is the gist of my humble advice about how to avoid such painful gaffes.

1. Just forge ahead with kindness. A young mother widowed on 9/11 told me it was great when people urged her to call if they needed anything, but it was even better when they took it upon themselves to offer to drive her kids to school or drop off poster board for the fourth-grade geography project. That spared her the discomfort of asking.

2. Be specific in what you propose. If you live near the clinic your friend is using, offer a room for a nap or an overnight stay after a treatment.

3. Stay connected. Patients often say people stop calling after the initial flurry of attention. Invite them to join you in the simple pleasures of

normal life, like going to a movie or watching a ball game.

4. If you can't think of something to say, try the old standby's like, "How 'bout them Mets?" Someone who is sick is not looking for a heavy conversation at every encounter and doesn't want to be defined only by his illness.

5. Resist the temptation to tell the patient's family about your brother-in-law or old college roommate who also has cancer, unless it's truly pertinent and useful. When everybody starts flooding you with cancer sagas, you end up drowning in sad stories.

6. Think twice before telling people to be positive. Dr. Jimmie C. Holland, the psycho-oncologist, railed against the "tyranny of positive thinking." When friends tell patients they should be optimistic, they imply that those who get sicker didn't try hard enough to stay upbeat or conquer the disease. That's unfair, and families should feel free to express anxiety and dark thoughts without being judged.

7. When words fail, just listen.

ESCAPE
October 2007

"There's a 6:00 p.m. flight to Paris," Elliot called from work to announce one September day. "Let's go."

We had barely unpacked from our family vacation in the Outer Banks. In the usual course of things we would wait a while to blow money on another big expedition. We were in journalism, after all, not banking. Our life was comfortable but frugal. I drove a car with 180,000 miles on it and never changed the ugly faux-pebble linoleum floor in our kitchen. Elliot resoled his work shoes instead of buying new ones. A hefty chunk of his paycheck went to his kids' college tuitions.

Some people assumed I was a trust fund baby. They were wrong. My parents were enormously generous in covering my children's educations but they would never support me. My father was a self-made man who believed handing grown children too much money "de-incentivized" them.

Elliot and I watched a tight budget and rationed out our trips. Until he got sick. Then we craved diversions. I didn't want to look back someday and regret denying him one of his few requests, an escape to his favorite city in the world. And who knew if I'd ever have another crack at a romantic getaway to Paris? There is a sense of urgency that comes with terminal illness, a what-the-hell impulsivity. My inner grasshopper stomped on my inner ant.

And so we booked a flight right after the next round of chemo.

On a crisp October afternoon we found ourselves having a late lunch by a window at Le Grand Colbert, a bistro near the Louvre, savoring one extravagant dish after another while the rest of the world was working. Elliot ignored some of his dietary restrictions and let himself have a glass of red wine, a rare indulgence since starting treatment fourteen months before. Perhaps it was the magic of Paris that he suffered no bad effects.

Every day of our week there Elliot put on a tweedy blue-gray jacket over a button-down shirt, the only time in our marriage he ever dressed up by choice, or for several days in a row. Now he wanted to treat this city, this art and this trip together with respect. There was, of course, the unspoken sense that it might be our last.

Elliot didn't have a long "bucket list" or any elaborate stunts in mind. Most of all, he simply wanted to be with our family and friends as much as possible. Beyond that, he talked about two other grand wishes. At some point, he wanted to take Aaron to Rome, because he'd taken Max a few years before, and he wanted to take Kate to Turkey. He loved leafing through travel books, typing up detailed itineraries and fantasizing about these adventures. We called it vacation foreplay.

Elliot had compiled such a guide for our trip. At the risk of sounding like a Philistine, I will confess that I wasn't crazy about his beloved museums and churches. They felt stuffy and claustrophobic. Nature stirs me more. But I wanted Elliot to do exactly what he wanted and figured I'd have the rest of my life, alas, to pick where to go. He took us to see one Madonna after another. Their wooden faces looked so stiff, so rigid, so blank—not at all how I'd look if I were grieving over my dead son. But then we saw one particular version of the Pieta. It wasn't the famous one by Michelangelo. I couldn't name the artist. I know only that it was impossible not to be moved as Mary looked down at the skeletal man lying limp in her arms, her face twisted in pure anguish. That will be me, I thought, my eyes stinging. And that will be Elliot.

Stop, I chided myself. He's here now. And we're in France. And we're in love, and that is enough.

We had a beautiful time. Perhaps the ache under the surface made every moment sweeter. There's a photo of Elliot sitting in the Luxembourg Gardens, where we had picnics of fresh baguettes, ham, brie and apricot tarts from the renowned Eric Kayser bakery. Elliot was adamant the croissants were the best in the universe. He looked like a hip professor with his gold-rimmed glasses and jacket over jeans. Sitting in a green metal chair with his legs crossed and a plastic cup of Pinot Noir in his hand, he looked utterly fulfilled.

He watched me drawing the statues in the park. I sketched the handsome naked ass of a Greek god on a pedestal and teased that it looked like his. We went shopping and he bought me black high heels that he always referred to as the "hot boots." We took long walks, revived at cafes and luxuriated in high quality naps before dinner and intimate desserts.

Our hotel on the left bank was simple, the Agora Saint Germain, near Notre Dame. Our room had a perfect view. The eighteenth century apartment building across the street had a little balcony where a pair of shiny black wetsuits had been hung out to dry. They told of two lovers who went on undersea adventures to explore fantastic things in mysterious places that nobody else got to see. I felt a certain kinship with that couple, whoever they were, and wished them well on their amorous escapades, as if they could have some on our behalf.

"I wish we had a movie of our week in Paris," Elliot wrote me after we got back. "It just goes by so fast."

Alex asks Elliot whether it's time to flip a pancake.

WAR AND PEACE AND PANCAKES

Back when we first got married, Elliot pulled out *The Joy of Cooking* and made pancakes from scratch one Saturday morning. He was trying to be nice, to make something special. Alex, a ridiculously picky eater, didn't want one.

"No thanks," he said.

"Oh come on," Elliot cajoled, his voice tinged with irritation that his well-meaning gesture was rejected. "If someone goes through the trouble of making you pancakes, it's only polite to give them a try."

This made my stomach tighten. I didn't want to undermine Elliot's good intentions, but I was raised in an Upper East Side apartment where the women were always on diets and it was considered a crime of monumental, possibly psyche-damaging insensitivity to force anyone to eat. Elliot grew up in a budget-conscious household where it was a sin to waste food. So he slapped a pancake onto the plates in front of each of my children at the breakfast table and then went back into the kitchen for coffee. Devon, mature beyond her seven years, forced it down to avoid hurting his feelings. Alex, only 4, looked at me with beseeching eyes.

"Do I have to?" he mouthed silently. I shook my head no, snuck his pancake onto my plate and wolfed it down before Elliot came back, though I didn't really want it either.

Stepfamilies can be complicated, full of small power plays and jealousies. Devon and Alex always liked Elliot's humor and warmth and boisterous commotion, but at times resented his powerful claim on my attention. I ached for them to love each other, and so was always trying to mediate, smooth things over, explain away what each party misunderstood. I had brought them together and felt it was my job to help them bond. For better or worse.

The next weekend, as Elliot got out the bowl to mix his batter, I gently suggested that maybe everyone could eat what he wanted at breakfast but Elliot continued undaunted, as if he'd win over Alex by sheer repetition.

This happened weekend after weekend, and Alex's resistance grew fiercer. I couldn't understand why Elliot was being so stubborn, creating a totally unnecessary conflict. My only guess was that he was trying to instill some manners in my loosey-goosey home or replicate the Saturday mornings of his past life with his kids, who apparently loved his pancakes. On mornings when Max was over for breakfast, it seemed to me that Elliot could make a batch just for him, but having all of us eat these pancakes became a matter of principle. Elliot's vision of family unity was about breaking the same bread together. Mine was of letting all of us happily do as we chose. After many months of this impasse, Elliot reluctantly accepted that his pancakes were causing a rift. He switched to French toast and running out for bagels, thank God, but this resolution came only after I spent too many Saturdays with pain in my gut from tension and secret consumption of Alex's portions. I was like the dog under the table, scarfing down the unwanted broccoli before the mom could see.

Maybe I was trying too hard. Maybe time would have worked its wonders without my determined diplomacy. Or maybe my careful mediations were effective.

All I know is that one Mother's Day, when my children were figuring out what to make for my traditional breakfast in bed, I heard Alex ask Elliot to teach him how to make pancakes. Alex was eight or nine by then. I lay back on my pillow and listened with the deepest satisfaction to the cheerful cacophony below as they collaborated in the kitchen, banging pots, washing blueberries and deciding who would run outdoors to find purple flowers to put in a tiny vase.

When Alex brought up my tray, careful not to spill the jug of maple syrup, he looked so pleased.

"Are they good?" he asked.

"Delicious," I said.

As soon as Alex was helping to make the pancakes, he realized he liked them too. Or maybe by that time he was just ready to concede. There's a photo from another Mother's Day when Alex has graduated to mixing the batter and manning the frying pan all by himself. He's standing at the stove in his black Mets T-shirt, spatula in hand, messy light brown hair spiked in every direction, looking up for a judgment as Elliot, in his white bathrobe, leans over to inspect the pancake for doneness. It is clear Alex has asked his opinion on whether it's time to flip. Elliot is considering the question with great intensity. It's one of my favorite photos, evidence of the deep connection that eventually evolved between them, even in an arena once so fraught with mutual annoyance.

Alex became quite the pancake king. That turned out to be a blessing. There came a time when Elliot could not get down anything dry, fatty or chewy. Pancakes became his go-to food, and he wanted them every day. Alex was his go-to chef.

"These are perfect, Mr. A," Elliot would say between bites. "Can I have another one, please?"

DOLPHINS
January 2008

The Jet Blue lounge in Newark was noisy, packed and smelly like moldy carpet. Elliot and I were about to escape for Martin Luther King Day weekend. As the months of treatment wore on, we became more and more dependent on such happy goalposts beckoning to us from the calendar on the kitchen wall. Once I read that farmhands worked more diligently in the fields if they had markers along each row to measure their progress. They were motivated by the promise that if they could just make it to the next marker, they could rest. And then the next marker, and the next. So as soon as we got back from Paris, I booked this trip to Florida for a few months later.

Getting to the airport marked a personal triumph. We were supposed to come exactly one year earlier, but ended up in the ER instead when Elliot got that horrible bile obstruction. When I called the owner of the bungalow place in Captiva back then, he said he'd give back my deposit.

"Please keep it," I told him. "We're going to find another time to come."

That was my vow that this obnoxious cancer wouldn't boss us around. Back in my twenties, when I had been a reporter at *The St. Petersburg Times* and walked these gorgeous Gulf of Mexico beaches alone, I had sworn I would come back someday with a man I loved. I refused to give up that dream.

As we waited for our flight to be called, I flipped through a magazine with glossy pictures of luxury island resorts. Our destination was much more low-key and low-budget. No pool, hot tub or tennis court, just a clean room on the bottom of a two-story house with a door that opened on to the white Florida sand and the bright turquoise water. Jensen's was owned by a family that also rented out cheap cabins next to a bait store on the bay side of the island, but I wanted to be on the Gulf, hearing the hypnotic crash of the waves.

"You know, Sweetie, this is a really simple place," I cautioned. "There won't be any amenities."

"You're my amenity," Elliot said with a grin. "All the amenity I need."

I scribbled his words down on the back of the white envelope that held our deposit receipt. It became a line in one of my periodic "good lists." I wrote them while I was waiting to meet Elliot in a restaurant, see a doctor, or pick up a child from a birthday party. My lists typically had the same format – everything good on one side of a column, everything bad on the other, so I could see how they balanced out and try to get some perspective. They helped me stay grounded and grateful for whatever was going well.

I was in a great mood heading off on vacation. Contrary to my usual format, this good list had no counterpoint "bad" list.

"Good list Jan 17, 2008" had seven entries:
- On the way to Captiva!
- Kids are doing well in school, have friends, are healthy, generally get along.
- Devon said "enough with turning new leaves and New Year's resolutions, you're doing fine." (After I resolved to spend more time one-on-one with each of the kids).
- I got a bonus for "Living with Cancer" stories.
- Elliot's going to Italy with Aaron in February—fun for him, break for me!
- He's so cute. Sees me writing this and says "I hope that's not work. That would be a violation."
- BOARDING NOW!!!

And so, exactly a year after our Captiva trip was originally supposed to happen, Elliot and I were settling into our seats on that flight to Sarasota, feeling giddy that we'd outfoxed fate.

It was too nippy for swimming, but we spent the days wandering along the sparkling water's edge, picking up shells, admiring the seagulls and laughing at the clumsy pelicans. I took a picture of Elliot when he was reading in our tiny screened in porch, bundled up in his bright red University of Wisconsin sweatshirt. By sheer luck the photo's lighting was perfect as he turned to smile at me, and the shot captured all the warmth, humor and sensitivity I saw in his face every day. In the photo he has Mona Lisa eyes too—they follow you wherever you stand. (I would one day use it for his memorial service, but I cropped out the book. I couldn't bear the irony of the title. It was Philip Roth's *Exit Ghost.*)

A few times on that trip we saw dolphins swimming just yards away. I remembered spotting dolphins in the far waves off Cape May, right after Elliot got sick, and thinking back then that it would be our last time seeing dolphins together. But here were some more playing right up close. Maybe their presence was proof we would keep enjoying pleasures I thought we had seen the last of, and I should stop obsessing about memorizing moments. Maybe there would be more than we thought, so we should just live them.

"I want to cram every possible opportunity into my life," Elliot said one day at dusk as we sat together on a bench watching the sun set over the water. "This is an important time for us. Maybe we'd prefer eighty-five degrees, but this is beautiful. I'm a very lucky man."

Later I wrote down Elliot's words on my envelope with the good list. No matter what the dolphins seemed to signify, I had to make sure I remembered.

WHEN IT RAINS...
Later in January 2008

All the cancer gurus insist that caregivers have to take care of themselves so they have the strength to take care of their patients. They cite the flight attendants' instructions on airplanes; put on your own oxygen mask before you help anyone else.

That's not easy. My main attempt was a yoga class at lunchtime on Wednesdays. A few work friends and I used to sneak off with our purple mats and almost always left our cell phones behind. I treasured that one hour of peace to breathe in, breathe out, relax.

One Wednesday soon after we got home from Captiva, I got back to my desk after yoga and saw my friend Bob rubbing his furrowed brow. His computer faced mine.

"Someone's been trying hard to reach you," he said with concern. My message light was bright red. With my heart pounding with worry that something new had gone wrong with Elliot, I dialed my password for voicemail.

It was Alex.

"Mommy, where ARE you?" his thin voice pleaded. He sounded so fragile, about to break. I called the school nurse, who said Alex had a stomachache and she'd sent him home with his father since she couldn't reach me.

"It hurts," Alex whimpered when I called him.

"I'm sorry, Sweetie," I said. "Just take it easy and let's see if you feel better."

Alex called back in twenty minutes.

"It really hurts," he insisted again. He sounded so strained, not himself. Something had to be really wrong.

Alex was not a complainer. Once when he was 4, he said he felt just a little sick and ended up in the ICU with an asthma attack. Another time, he seemed a little stuffed up and it turned out he had pneumonia. Once again, it seemed there was no time to waste. I asked Milo to take Alex to the pediatrician and I jumped in the car to meet them. I was almost there when my cell phone rang again.

"The doctor says it might be appendicitis and we should get it checked out at the hospital just in case," Milo said. "We'll meet you at Morristown Memorial."

Morristown was thirty minutes away. Milo was a fast driver but not good with directions. I pictured Alex writhing in the back seat while Milo got lost in traffic. Damn it. I'm the expert at speeding to the ER, I thought. I knew how to get there. Alex should be with me.

I have always felt extra protective of my little boy. My daughter seemed older than her years, and shrewd. My son always seemed a bit young and tender with his freckles, deep dimples and impish smile. Even his big sister said he was cute. He was late to develop his Rs so at eleven he still sounded a bit like a Rugrat. His wild hair stuck out in all directions and I rarely forced him to brush it. I let him do what he pleased with his crazy hair partly because he had so little say over so much in his life. He was so young when his father and I split up and I always felt guilty about that. The kids got used to it in time, and it was for the best, but still.

Guilt pangs hit again as I drove like hell to the hospital, trying to execute those yoga breaths to stay calm, telling myself if anything was truly dire the pediatrician would have called an ambulance. I had been so focused on Elliot, but now, my son was the one who needed me.

At the ER, Alex and Milo were nowhere to be seen. I checked frantically with the nurses and reception desk. I paced outside the ER door. Damn it damn it damn it.

Finally they showed up. Yes, they'd gotten lost. Alex was in a wheelchair, grimacing and doubled over. He looked petrified.

"It's okay, Sweetie, everything's going to be fine," I cooed.

"Can't you give him anything?" I begged the triage nurse while she took down his information. "He's in pain."

"Not until the doctor sees him," she said.

We were ushered into a chilly little room with a high narrow gurney. I peeled off Alex's Mets hoodie and tried to put on a gown without hurting him. He was squirming so much the blanket kept falling off. His bare legs looked so vulnerable. Lying on his side in a fetal curl, he started to pant instinctively with those quick shallow breaths they teach you in Lamaze. He put his hot hand out for me to hold.

"Can't you please give him something for the pain?" I pleaded. The staff seemed to be moving like molasses and my little boy was in agony. Doctors threw pain meds at my husband like it was candy. Couldn't somebody please give relief to my son?

"If this turns out to be some kind of spasm then morphine will make it worse," the doctor said. Alex's squirming seemed to contradict a "classic presentation" of appendicitis, when it hurts too much to move. "We have to wait for a CT scan before we give him anything. Try putting on a video so he can relax."

We put on an action-packed football melodrama, *Remember the Titans*, but Alex couldn't pay attention. He winced and squeezed my hand and said those words it kills you to hear when there's nothing you can do.

"Mommy, help me. Please…"

"I'm so sorry, Sweetie. You'll get through this and it will feel much better. I'm so proud of you. What a trouper."

"Mommy, it hurts so much, I can't," he whimpered.

His next question knocked the wind out of me.

"Do I have cancer?"

"Oh, Sweetie-Pie." I leaned over to hug him and kiss him and tell him no, don't worry.

"But it's my stomach, just like with Elliot."

"Oh Honey, it's really rare for kids to get cancer," I told him, brushing the sweaty hair off his forehead. "The doctors think maybe it's your appendix, and then they can fix that really easily. Everything's going to be just fine."

I stayed confident on the outside—my son needed that, and eighteen months of nursing my husband had given me plenty of practice—but inside I didn't feel calm at all. It was startling to me that Alex had cancer on his mind this way. I had tried so hard to keep things as normal as possible for my kids and say all the right comforting things. For my son to think he might have cancer meant Elliot's ordeal was on his mind far more than I realized. Not only that, the same unfathomable idea had occurred to me too: what if Alex did have cancer? I told myself that was farfetched. I had to believe that some kind of cosmic sense of decency wouldn't allow such a meteor to hit my husband and my son at the same time. Then again, I'd met a woman my age, a cashier at a K-Mart, juggling shifts so she could drive her husband and daughter to Sloan-Kettering in a relentless rotation of IVs and nausea. Please not that, I begged the godless air. I squeezed Alex's hand to reassure him, and myself.

The nurse came in with a giant pitcher of an awful chalky drink Alex had to swallow before the CT scan.

He could barely sit up to suck a straw. Somehow he sipped the disgusting stuff, tiny bit by bit. I marveled at his persistence. Almost done. And then in one big push he leaned over the side of the bed and threw up.

"Please don't tell me he has to start over," I asked the nurse.

"No, he's still got most of it."

Finally a doctor gave him a little morphine and he grew still enough for the CT scan. It was his appendix after all. Surgery was scheduled for 5:30 in the morning, just few hours away.

Alex and I were sent upstairs to the pediatric floor. Milo would come back for the operation. Elliot was home with Devon. A pretty nurse brought me a sheet and pillow and helped me unfold the vinyl chair-bed next to Alex's bed. I lay down to keep vigil yet again next to one of my sweet warriors.

The surgery went well. I could breathe. As soon as Alex woke up, his main concern was keeping the gruesome appendage for show and tell. Not a chance. We settled in to spend another night while he recovered.

"I'm sorry you have to stay with me after all your nights in the hospital with Elliot," Alex said earnestly. My heart swelled at his compassion. We must be doing something right, I thought.

"Oh Honey, there's nothing I'd rather do," I said. "I mean, I'd much rather you weren't sick, but if you're here this is exactly where I want to be."

The routine pediatric ward was nothing like a cancer unit. For patients feeling well enough, there was a mischievous sense of playing hooky, with a vending machine that spat out videos for free. Alex and his sixteen-year-old roommate, Kyle with a broken leg from a daredevil ski accident, spent hours jamming on Guitar Hero. That slow day was a welcome respite.

The most peaceful part of it all was that there was absolutely no question about where I should be. My place was here with my son, fetching him water, helping him out of bed, getting the nurse if he needed painkillers. Ever since Elliot got sick, there was a nagging tension about how to balance my time, how to make sure I was supporting him through the trial of his life while not neglecting my kids, who, after all, would be little for only an instant. On Saturday mornings, when Elliot wanted me to read the paper with him for hours, Alex wanted me to drive him to a friend's or football. When Elliot was feeling well enough to schlep to a museum but the kids wanted to hang out at home, I'd feel torn.

Now, for the first time in a long while, the family wasn't revolving around Elliot.

To my delight, Elliot dove into his sudden new role as caregiver with gusto. After Devon got out of school, he brought her to visit. They carried a big duffel bag full clothes, pajamas, toiletries and books. It was a kick to have Elliot pack for me for a change, to have him tend to the needs of the ones stuck in the hospital. He gave Alex *ESPN* magazines and a baseball glove made out of gold lamé inscribed "You're a Champ."

"I miss you," Elliot whispered when he kissed me goodbye. "I can't sleep without you."

That night I smiled to myself as I settled down to sleep next to another man for the first time in a very long while. Alex's roommate's father, a National Guardsman on break from Iraq, had decided to stay over as well, and lay down on another fold-out chair squeezed into the room. I couldn't believe how loudly the guy snored. I don't know how his wife put up with it.

A LETTER FROM ELLIOT
On the eve of his trip to Italy with Aaron

Thursday, Feb. 21, 2008

Leslie, my beautiful girl…

I'm just about all packed now for Rome, all my meds and maps and insane itineraries, and tucked away in there I have a little piece of you hidden among the T-shirts and sweaters, a photo from Paris, you caught sketching at the Luxembourg Gardens, looking as lovely and fetching as you did that first day you walked into *The Record* newsroom and I thought to myself, "Boy, some lucky guy is married to *her*."

Somehow, I became that guy, and a whole new life opened up for me. The kind of life I dreamed of when I was starting out on my own, when I left New York for Wisconsin filled with a lot of naïve, romantic ideas about finding someone sweet and smart to love and care about, and yes, pretty too, I'm not ashamed to admit it.

I appreciate beauty in art, in music, in nature, why wouldn't I want beauty in my life every day, someone to love and lust after, to adore and look up to? You've given me that, and now that I have you, I can't imagine a life, my life, without all that.

You should know that I've never taken along a photo like the one I just packed. It's not just that I'll miss you terribly, which is obvious—your physical presence, the feel of you in bed next to me, honestly, I don't know how I can eat breakfast without you there—and it worries me because in the past year-and-a-half I've felt much closer to you than I ever thought possible—a wonderful thing—and more dependent, a burden which weighs on you terribly, I know.

I wish that part weren't so.

It's you that's kept me alive through all this, all the love and care you've given me, the hard work you've done and the stress you've endured, just to get me and us through my situation, as we've come to call it…

From the moment you came into my life—when does it start, where do you count from precisely—your first appearance in the newsroom? DYFS? That goodbye at your car?

It's all a jumble to me now, I can't reconcile the chronology. I just know that somewhere over those days and weeks and months, slowly and irrefutably, I started to feel something overwhelming that roused me from an existence without love or desire or purpose other than my kids.

And now I have you, and I don't know any other way to live. There is so much sweetness and love and caring in my life, that I can't bear the thought of being without you. Which is why I put up with the bi-weekly trips into the city, the dreadful drugs, the dark cloud that follows me around.

Because I know that for all that, that every day holds the possibility of something beautiful and loving, whether it's the corner room at the Old Inn on the Green or Room 310 at the University Club, whether it's Paris or Montclair.

I have a beautiful life and you to thank for it.

I love you every day…

Elliot

HOW TO SLEEP WITH YOUR HUSBAND
IN A HOSPITAL BED
May 2008

Hospitals must rank among the hardest places to sleep.

Besides the fluorescent lighting and 5:00 a.m. blood draws, doctors' pagers go off. The nurses get alerts from robotic voices crackling from walkie-talkies hung around their necks. Heavy food carts rumble by and the wheels on IV poles squeak as patients push them on laps around the unit. Sometimes you hear the most miserable among them groan, cough or spit. Once a woman who arrived at the threshold of her husband's room screamed and collapsed sobbing on the linoleum floor. Two orderlies hoisted her onto a plastic chair and dragged it scraping to a conference room so she could recover.

It was May, and Elliot was back in the hospital. After he got back from a fabulous trip to Italy with his son, the cancer had spread to a muscle near his pelvis. Radiation was ordered. He'd never had that before. It was an outpatient procedure, ten doses over two weeks, but in the middle of the series a blood test revealed he had a serious infection. So we were making ourselves at home on Sloan-Kettering's sixteenth floor. Again.

Gone were my newbie days of pushing together two stiff wooden chairs at night, sitting on one and hooking my feet on the other. I had discovered the joys of the recliners. The trick was grabbing one and keeping it. Competition was stiff. It was heartening to find that in this harsh world, where dysfunctional marriages and domestic violence seemed to get all the press, there were still plenty of husbands and wives who wanted to stay overnight with the spouses they adored. There was a certain bonding among those of us who were healthy. We nodded to each other as we passed in the hallway in the morning on the way to brushing our teeth, like we were all on a strange kind of camp out. I was extremely fortunate to know my kids always had a happy place to stay with their dad when I stayed with Elliot in the hospital. Alex always sent his teddy bear to keep Elliot company. It had a Mets logo on one paw and made for a good ice breaker with the nurses.

If I was lucky enough to score one of the precious recliners, I'd wheel it next to Elliot's bed. I'd wake up from a short nap with my cheek stuck to the vinyl cushion. I was loath to bother the nurses as they rushed around but there were aides who could satisfy my timid requests for sheets, a towel or some soap.

At some point I realized it felt even better to both of us if I just squeezed into bed with him. I didn't dare do that if he had an IV line in both arms, or if he might have a tender spot from a stent procedure, but otherwise I climbed right in. It was a tight fit so I hitched up the guardrails to keep from falling out. I buried my face in his warm, salty neck and kissed his shoulder where his skin peeked out between the snaps of his hospital gown. Sometimes he couldn't move much but would turn his head to kiss my hair. There was sheer animal comfort in lying against each other. At least our arms and legs could feel skin on skin.

Staying with him wasn't about obligation. It was simply where I wanted to be. There is a special tenderness when one of you could choose to go, but you stay where your heart is. We were going through this together, and felt closer than ever.

It was an awfully public setting for such intimacies, but we didn't really care. We wanted as much of each other as we could get. We couldn't exactly make love but we could make do. Spooning has its unique rewards, and our hands could travel all kinds of places under the covers. Nurses joked about the newlyweds.

Sometimes only a thin curtain separated us from a roommate. One night the patient on the other side of the drapery was a Jesuit Father. I boasted to friends that I had just slept with a priest.

My nightwear became increasingly brazen. At first I'd wear a sweatshirt and yoga pants. That way I'd be covered up when doctors came in. That outfit got hot, though, so in time I cut down to a tank top and yoga pants. Over time that shifted to just a T-shirt and underwear. I figured doctors had seen it all anyway, and I was too tired to care, and if they got a thrill from seeing a worried wife's panties, let 'em have it.

Because worry was always simmering under the surface smiles, worry was why I slept with Elliot during almost every one of his dozens of overnight hospital stays, except for a few when I thought I'd fall apart if I didn't catch up on real rest.

We were both afraid that if I left him to sleep by himself, Elliot might die alone.

Leslie, Alex, Devon, Elliot and Max hiking in the Adirondacks, Summer 2008.

THE PEACH
Summer 2008

Radiation didn't do much good, and Elliot's second pair of chemotherapies had stopped working. We talked about an out-of-date drug used by a woman I'd interviewed for the newspaper series who claimed to have accomplished the extraordinary feat of living fourteen years after a diagnosis of inoperable pancreatic cancer.

"It's like that scene in *When Harry Met Sally*," Elliot said. "I'll have what she's having."

He could joke but he was losing his capacity to protect himself through denial. The tumor near his pelvis hurt like a knife slicing down his thigh. He needed increasingly high-powered meds to get comfortable. We spent hours one day in the waiting room of the pain management clinic. I have never seen such a miserable bunch. There was a woman with a chunk missing from her jaw, a man doubled-over in agony in his wheelchair. I thought they should start an anti-smoking version of those "Scared Straight" programs, which used to take juvenile delinquents to prisons to show them how wretched their lives would be if they kept up with their drugs, gangs and crime. Of course I don't know if smoking had anything to do with these patients' conditions, but if I ever caught my kids with cigarettes, I'd bring them straight to this clinic for a preview of what might happen. Elliot couldn't help leaving that place depressed.

He'd seen a Sloan-Kettering psychiatrist a few times since getting sick but didn't want to go anymore. He didn't like the way counseling stirred up dark visions about the realities ahead. When he put off making appointments, I was disappointed. It was a daunting responsibility for me to be the only vessel for his deepest anxieties.

Elliot was more open about his despair in his writing than he admitted out loud.

"I've lost the ability to believe there's a good reason to be hopeful," he emailed me one day in May.

"What makes me so sad," he wrote in June, "is that there was so much I wanted to do with you, so many places I wanted us to see together. I wanted to see my kids happy with what they were doing in life."

"I looked in the mirror and now more than ever I look like a guy with cancer," he wrote another day. It embarrassed him to look that way at the office. "I can't stand it. And my pants are falling off me. I have to walk around with my hands in my pockets to hold them up. I'm eating everything I can but can't seem to make a dent."

On the outside he tried to act like things were going well. He even lobbied for, and got, a plum new assignment at *Bloomberg*. It was a dream job for him, editing stories about arts and culture. It had a key side benefit— a much slower pace than legal news and an editor who encouraged him to work from home as much as he needed, which was becoming all the time. He polished up colorful stories about theatre directors, art shows, wine auctions and European spas. He even edited a piece declaring that the hot new trend in men's pants was the "drop-crotch."

"Who knew," I teased, "that you would be so fashionable?"

We tried, sometimes, to make light of things but it was difficult for me to look at him naked. His ribs showed like an Auschwitz prisoner's. His upper arms had lost much of their muscle. They were actually thinner than mine. His thighs were so skinny that his white briefs drooped loosely around them like badly pinned diapers.

"Don't mourn him now," I told myself, again and again. "You'll have plenty of time for that later."

My pep talks to myself cycled on a relentless loop. Just a hundred years ago a man was lucky to live to be forty-five, so compared to most of human history he's ahead of the game. At least he's not a soldier dying on a battlefield without morphine. At least he's not seven years old. At least we have insurance. At least I have a flexible part-time job so I can take care of him. At least we found each other. So many people go through their lives without a love like this.

I got sick of my own cajoling voice in my head. A therapist once told me I was afraid of anger. I think I was also afraid of grief—that if I gave in to it I would crumble. I would be sucked into a bottomless pit and would never come back out. So I steeled myself with smiles and tried to focus on what we still had. I didn't want to look back on these days and kick myself for wasting them in sorrow. These were the good days. I had to appreciate them because I knew it would get so much worse.

"Don't be afraid to get closer," the social worker had said. "He's here now."

Maybe bottling up my distress served a good purpose. I didn't, after all, fall apart. I kept our house and family running like a finely calibrated machine.

My main goal was to squeeze in as many fun times with our children as possible. We had booked rooms for all seven of us, plus Kate's boyfriend, at the Hedges in the Adirondacks, a rustic cluster of cabins surrounding Blue Mountain Lake. Getting away always made us feel better. In June we piled into a rented minivan that would fit all of us along with board games, Frisbees, baseball gloves, books and piles of pills. Somehow Elliot managed to hike up two mountains in the drizzling rain, stopping every minute or so to catch his breath. Going so slowly we found pleasures in the path that we might otherwise have missed—tiny red lizards, hummingbirds and mushrooms in wildly phallic shapes. The lake was too cold for swimming, but we kayaked, read in rocking chairs on the porch and had campfires in the dark. There's a picture of Alex and Max laughing as they wrestle on a worn plaid couch in our cabin. It was the first time I'd seen them tussle like puppies. Like brothers.

One day Elliot and Alex bought some cheap fishing poles, caught some big ones and threw them back. One time it took so long to pull the hook out of a trout's mouth that we thought we killed it so we took it to the kitchen to cook for dinner. Soon after the fish hit the ice bucket it started twitching and sprang back to life. Wouldn't that be nice, I thought. A second chance…

"I wish we were still up in Blue Mountain Lake, just you and me," Elliot emailed me a few days after we got back. "I'll bet we could get the Colonel's room for a few days, say Sunday thru Wednesday. I just want to spend the day in bed. Happy Anniversary."

It was our eighth. Where had the time gone?

One night back home in July I found Elliot in our room in his underwear, dancing to the thrum of the air conditioner.

"Are you doing that to amuse me or because you're moved by the music?" I asked.

"Both," he said with a grin. It was funny but gave me a chill. He was loopy from all the pain medicines, Fentanyl and Lyrica on top of everything else.

He felt isolated working at home so he kept trying to schlep into the office, but commuting was getting harder. "I have to navigate the trains, the streets, on new, more powerful meds," he wrote. "I feel more than a little disoriented and my reaction time feels slow. Believe me, I'm not challenging cars to cross the street…I'm just woozy, and woozy is not the best armor for surviving in New York."

He sounded so wistful sometimes. "I'm looking at the picture I took of you in Maine…that summer we rented the house near Popham Beach. You look so fetching. I can't concentrate on anything else…"

How I loved those emails. I was addicted to their ardor. I hated to envision a time I would have to get by without them. Stop it, I told myself. Don't go there.

We had a trip for two planned on the way to picking up Alex from camp in New Hampshire in August. We stopped for a few days at our favorite bed and breakfast, the Old Inn on the Green in New Marlborough, Massachusetts. We took long walks, long baths and long naps. We visited our friend Linda's country house nearby. She and her fiancé had an orchard and we picked a perfect peach. It was so beautiful we couldn't bear to eat it. For days we just admired it on the mantel by our bed at the inn. I splurged on a forty-five dollar set of colored pencils just so I could sketch that lovely piece of fruit. I spent hours on its portrait while Elliot slept. Looking carefully at the peach's delicate round shape, with its soft oranges, pinks and greens, was so calming that I felt time slow down. My breath got softer. It was almost like meditation. I felt a rare sense of peace in that room, with my husband resting and my whole body relaxed.

It struck me that the day marked the two-year anniversary of Elliot's diagnosis. His doctors had predicted that by this time he probably wouldn't be with us anymore. But he was still here with me, and we were happy.

I'm proud of my drawing that day, it came out well. And once it was finished, we bit into that idyllic peach. It was the sweetest, juiciest one I had ever tasted. It dribbled down our chins and we licked away its nectar with the purest kind of contentment. We live for moments like this.

The next day we spent a glorious sunny afternoon biking around Lake Winnapesaukee, fantasizing about the houses we would buy someday. Who would think a man in Elliot's condition could do that? Maybe we could carry on like this for a long while, I thought, ricocheting between emergency rooms and romantic adventures. Maybe we had much more time than the doctors ever thought.

On good days we were determined to be cheerful. Sometimes Max and Kate brought over their Lhasa Apso, Mookie, to keep Elliot company when he was working from home. Alex was tickled to come into the kitchen one day to find Elliot dancing around with Mookie in his arms, singing old show tunes.

When we were exhausted, though, despair could creep its way in.

"I'm so tired," Elliot wrote from his office in late August. "I just felt like I was going to collapse…and I hate limping around here at work. I feel so conspicuous. I hate it."

"I love you," I wrote back. That was all I could think of to say. I refused to lie or spout false optimism. Anything fake would feel like a wall between us.

"I can't keep limping around here. I won't do that. I feel like I have a sign around my neck that says cancer patient."

The pain specialist kept upping the doses. They made Elliot so drowsy that he started to fall asleep as soon as we started kissing at night. Elliot was crushed but determined to fix the problem. It affected the core of his sense of self as a man. I loved that he still cared so passionately about this kind of connection, and it amazed me that it took so long for his mountains of drugs to get in the way. He soldiered on, unwavering in his mission to find opportunities to please. He refused to give up life's greatest rewards.

"I'm feeling a bit lightheaded, edgy, but the methadone seems to have blunted the pain substantially, so how can I complain?" he emailed me one day. "Only problem is that… 'other problem,' which I'm confident we can overcome with time and patience. Because as powerful as these meds are, my love for you is stronger by far. I think you knew that…"

One day Elliot forgot his jacket on the train, fell down the station stairs and almost stepped into the gap between the subway and the platform. It was clear he was getting too spacey for the commute. I kept suggesting that if he didn't like to work at home, we should find a carpool or hire a taxi. It turned out *Bloomberg* would pay for one, but he didn't want to be treated like an invalid. His obstinacy was an asset in fighting this disease but it could also keep him from accepting practical solutions.

Elliot clung to the shards of denial as much as he could. I couldn't afford to. As much as I wanted to stay in the present, and appreciate every minute of our time together, I had to think ahead too. I was the one who made sure we updated our wills and health care proxies. I was the one who had to calculate whether I could stay in our house with my kids on just my income. I was the one who Googled articles on helping kids cope with bereavement because I'd be the one left behind to deal with their devastation. I was the one who might need to initiate getting help from hospice; he would never make that move. It would signal giving up. I thought about doing some research on local hospices just in case, maybe even writing a newspaper article about them as a way to check out a few places, but that seemed sneaky. If I went scouting out deathbeds behind Elliot's back, and he found out about it, he would be shattered.

"Hope for the best," my doctor told me at a checkup, "but prepare for the worst."

When Elliot's third pair of chemo drugs failed to help, he agreed to try an experimental one. Until now he was reluctant to be a "guinea pig" but had no real options left. He was scheduled to start a trial of a pill called Brevanib in mid-September.

"How many more ways can I show/tell you I love you?" he slugged an email in early September. "I'm drifting off again. But you're all I think about lately. Well, you and that pill I'll be taking in a week or so. But I try not to think about that, so more/most of my thoughts are amorous ones about you. We should hop a plane to Paris, book a week at the Agora Saint Germain, line up in the morning at Eric Kayser's boulangerie, and while away the afternoons at the Luxembourg Gardens or the Grand Palais, leave time for a nap (definitely!) then dinner at Les Pipos. I see the Louvre, the Musee d'Orsay and the Picasso Museum are collaborating on a massive Picasso show that runs from October till February of next year. He's not my favorite, but in small doses, and certain periods, I do enjoy."

Elliot had always reveled in his vivid fantasy life. At least he still had that.

CELEBRATION
September 2008

"It is always like this: The best parties are thrown by people in trouble."

Amy Bloom, *Away*

The doctors didn't say how bad things were getting, and Elliot didn't ask, but it was clear. So I decided to throw a party.

I am my mother's daughter that way. In a crisis, she opts for diversion. Once when I was little we got into a jam on my parents' sailboat. The wind died and the engine failed and we couldn't get out of a dangerous spot in a tricky harbor. The Coast Guard officers who came to tow us to safety must have been baffled to find that while we were waiting to be rescued, my mother had put out wine and cheese.

There was more to my party plan than mere distraction. I kept thinking of a friend at work, Pat Gilbert, a young mother who had died several years earlier. So many people came to her funeral—reporters, neighbors, relatives—and it seemed such a shame that all these friends who cared about her were there, but the one person who connected them all was not. I couldn't bear the idea that someday all the people who loved Elliot might be gathered in one room without him. If they were going to come together for his sake, I wanted Elliot to be there, and I wanted him to enjoy it.

I envisioned something warm and casual but classy, with good food and music that allowed for real conversation. My hands were too full to cook for a crowd, but Taro was the right size for about sixty people. We could take over the whole restaurant. It had a calm space with elegant bamboo stalks stretching up to its high ceiling, white tablecloths with pink and purple flowers, and gold candlelight reflecting off mirrors. That's where we ate a few nights after Elliot's diagnosis, when I'd seen a couple on an awkward first date and hoped to the highest heavens that I'd never be in that position again.

Of course I couldn't couch this party as a pre-funeral. I pitched it to Elliot as a thank-you dinner for all the friends who had helped us for so long, bringing us dinners, driving the kids, making us laugh. I was sincere in my gratitude; it wasn't only a ruse, and he smiled at the idea. Even so, he divined my deeper motivation. When I asked him if he wanted to have toasts, he shook his head no.

"Save the eulogies," he said.

It was hard to settle on a date. I was eager to have the party as soon as possible, but so many friends were away on summer vacation that hosting it in late August seemed to defeat the purpose. I wondered what kind of shape Elliot would be in if we held off until September but waiting seemed worth the risk. I booked Taro for an early dinner on the first Sunday after Labor Day. Unfortunately Max would be back in Ithaca by then, but I didn't think this could be delayed until his fall break in October.

We sent out sky blue invitations with a big maroon "thanks" in the middle. Practically everyone we invited said yes. They understood my intent. I think many were touched by such a tangible gesture of appreciation. People are starving for signs they are truly valued. My one regret was that I couldn't invite my loyal book club buddies and their husbands too, but that would add sixteen people, and Elliot was starting to feel intimidated by the size of the guest list.

I went to Taro one morning to discuss the menu with the manager, Charlie, a balding Chinese man whose face was lined with deep wrinkles. I got fixated on fretting about how eight large tables should be arranged around the room. I wanted to be certain that during first hour of appetizers and drinks, there would be space for people to mingle.

"Don't worry," Charlie said. "We've done this many times before. It will be fine."

I almost kissed the man. When was the last time anyone had said "don't worry" to me? It was a relief to leave the details to him, to delegate, to trust it really would work out. All I had to do was provide the music and dessert.

That would be easy. Baking was Kate's forte. She always made such incredible grand finales for family holidays – a tart piled with raspberries and blackberries, homemade gelato with spiced walnuts, or everybody's all-time favorite, pumpkin bread pudding laced with chocolate. Her best recipes were her own inventions.

"How would you feel about making dessert for this party?" I asked her. "About sixty people? I know that's a lot of work."

"Sure," she said without hesitation.

"Thank you so much. It will mean so much to Elliot. And to me."

This party became a whole family effort. Kate's boyfriend, Anthony, helped us find a jazz guitarist. Aaron, who flew in from Chicago with his girlfriend, Sallie, for the occasion, drove to Washington Heights to pick up Elliot's mother. Devon volunteered to take pictures. Alex agreed to take care of the one little boy who would be there. I found out later that Elliot's first wife, to her great credit, helped Kate finish making mountains of apple pastries, chocolate walnut tarts and blondies, even though she wasn't invited. It would have felt awkward to have Janet there, but she contributed nonetheless.

It was a swell party. Elliot looked tan and handsome in a loose blue plaid linen shirt that hid his bony ribs. His face shined with delight as friends came over for a hug or a handshake or a pat on the back.

"Hey, Elliot," said one after another. "You look good."

As we all sat down to Chilean sea bass, coconut shrimp and filet mignon, I found my spot next to my husband and took a moment to survey the tables. Everyone was clinking wine glasses, catching up and laughing.

Many were journalists abuzz with the weekend's news that Lehman Brothers was about to file for bankruptcy. The global financial markets were about to implode, but all I cared about was celebrating that we'd made it this far. Most of the time we'd lived awfully well. I felt a warm rush of awe at the enormous generosity of these friends who had helped us get through so much.

There were Maggie and John, who mailed us the keys to their country house in Little Compton, Rhode Island, so we could escape to the ocean for a weekend. There was Linda, who, the minute she heard we were bored with the DVD shelf at the chemo clinic, Fed Exed the whole first season of *Mad Men*. There was Henry, who entertained Elliot at work with a running series of emails that were sympathetic, amusingly kvetchy and risqué. There were my editors who let me switch my work days around willy-nilly whenever I wanted to accommodate kids or medical crises. There were friends who picked up Elliot's prescriptions in the city, or took him to baseball games, or gave me bubble bath when I seemed on the verge of collapse. And there were the ones who were simply always with us, like Pam, Dick, Lynn and Robert.

There was my sister too. There had been times when we weren't as close as we both would have liked but she absolutely stepped up to the plate when Elliot got sick. She checked on us by phone and visited when she could. Once, a few months before this party, I called her in exhausted depression.

"I'm knocking myself out taking care of Elliot and what is it going to get me?" I whined. "Nothing. One day all this will end and I'll be alone. Then what am I going to do? So I'm a good cancer wife, big deal. I can't exactly put that on my resume."

"I don't see it that way at all," Jessie said calmly. "What could possibly be more important than taking care of someone you love who needs you? What is more meaningful than that?"

Hearing her say that meant so much to me. I appreciated the way she kept calling to let me vent. Because that's the thing with cancer. It can drag on an awfully long time. It's the true blue friends who keep calling and cooking and coming by. They don't shy away. They don't assume they will be intruding.

"Don't be afraid to get closer," the social worker had told me. The friends in this restaurant had lived by her words without ever hearing them. There was a certain grace in their collective spirit of kindness. It felt profound, and authentic, and made my heart full.

"You could feel the outpouring of love in that room," Linda wrote me later. There was pride too. Elliot's mother beamed at the sight of so many people who had driven from Pennsylvania, Delaware and Connecticut to join us. Even at her age, a mother loves to see that her child has good friends. Elliot was proud of Kate's desserts. And I was proud to see my children and his all staked out seats together even though the older ones could have split off to eat with grownup family friends. They made for a cute kiddie table.

Near the end of dinner, Elliot and I stood up to say a few words. Devon caught Elliot's on video.

"My shrink says the trick to this is finding the balance between hope and depression," he said slowly, carefully, looking down shyly.

("Elliot sees a shrink?" Alex's voice asks in the background.)

"Everyone in this room," Elliot continued, "has helped me do that in one way or another. So thank you, all of you."

WHERE'S ROGER?
October 2008

We were so used to talking, joking and writing emails to each other that I worried some kind of distance might grow between us if we lost that verbal connection, if his mind became foggy. It was a terrible thing to see looming.

A preview came one Sunday night in October. We were having dinner at Beacon, a sleek restaurant off Fifth Avenue, after seeing *Speed the Plow*, a David Mamet play about manipulative Hollywood agents. I'd gotten tickets to take our minds off the next morning's Sloan-Kettering appointment, when we would find out whether Elliot's liver could tolerate more chemotherapy. Good news seemed unlikely.

The waiter pushed the prix fixe dinner that started with a sizzling plate of a half-dozen roasted oysters. They smelled garlicky and delicious, and since they were cooked we ignored our usual concern about exposing Elliot to the potential germs in shellfish. We ate them all with gusto. Then the steak course came. Halfway through, Elliot looked around the table.

"Where are the oysters?" he asked suddenly.

"We had them," I answered, puzzled.

"Really?" He paused. "Huh."

We kept eating.

"Where's Roger?" he asked, his brow knit in confusion. We hadn't seen his old friend in over a year. There was absolutely no reason for Roger to show up that night.

"I'm not sure, Sweetie," I said. "Maybe he's at home."

When we finished, I reached for the check—who knew what bizarre thing Elliot might write if he tried to sign the bill. As spacey as he was, he still questioned my calculation of the tip. That made me smile, but

I was nervous. As we walked back to our hotel, Eriq La Salle, the tall black actor who played a sullen loner of a surgeon on *ER* for years, passed by. I wondered what he would tell me to do, as if he had any medical know-how in real life.

The next morning Elliot seemed lucid again, but he took forever to shower and dress. His leg hurt as he hobbled toward the outpatient clinic. His stomach was roiling. There was little I could do to but hold his hand.

"I wanted to make love to you so much this weekend," Elliot said. "What happened? The days just slipped by. I was so tired. I love you. That's one thing I can say. I've said it a million times."

We had to wait forever to see the doctor. He had bad news.

"The tumor is not so well controlled," he said in a blatant euphemism. He wanted another CT scan within a week.

We begged the scheduler to squeeze in Elliot that afternoon so we wouldn't have to make a return trip to the city. Luckily there was an opening at 2:00 p.m. In the waiting room I flipped through irritatingly cheerful magazines—"flat abs in thirty days!"— and couldn't focus. The CT scan was taking more than an hour, much longer than usual. School was over so I called home to check on the kids. They were arguing about whose turn it was to unload the groceries that had just been delivered. Such banal minutia offered a welcome escape.

Anxious to get home before dinner, I pushed my way into the CT scan suite to find out what was taking so long.

"There's a blood clot in his lung," a nurse said. "The radiologist has to look at past scans to see if it's a new one."

It was. Of course.

"You need to go to Urgent Care at the main hospital," the radiologist said. "Now."

Elliot rolled his eyes in disgust. He was so sick of this. Me too.

On Third Avenue I waved my arms wildly to hail a cab. One swerved over and before I could stop him Elliot marched around to the far side of the taxi and opened the door into oncoming traffic. Another cab almost hit him. Our driver exploded in a venomous tirade in an unknown language and then switched to English.

"You can't get in that side," he barked. "I could lose my license!"

Please, I begged the driver, just take us to the hospital. Please, I begged Elliot, be careful. Between exhaustion, drugs and whatever new was going wrong inside, Elliot was too uncoordinated to venture into city streets on his own. He didn't want to believe it.

"You need to listen to me," I snapped as we sped uptown. "You're not exactly at the top of your game."

"Maybe that would be the best thing," he shot back. "I'll just get hit by a bus and get it over with."

He rarely talked about giving up. I kissed him hard to silence him.

"We'll get through this," I insisted.

So there we were back in the waiting room at Urgent Care yet again, our sixth time, smelling the odd mix of alcohol wipes, floor bleach and Chinese take-out. A television on the wall showed CNN reporters babbling breathlessly about the stock market. The Dow had plunged 800 points that day. It was the beginning of the economy's downward spiral.

"The public mood is grim," the anchor declared soberly. We watched news of the nation's financial panic for distraction from our real problems.

We spent hours, as usual, waiting for a room to be ready upstairs. Finally, around 10:00 p.m. we got in the elevator to the sixteenth floor. Elliot's forehead felt warm to my lips.

By the time we got to his room, he was starting to sound out of it again, like the night before at dinner. I called in the nurse. Apparently he'd spiked a fever since leaving the ER downstairs. She called for the resident, stat.

"What year is it, Mr. Pinsley?" the young doctor asked nervously.

"What month is it?"

"Do you know where you are?"

Elliot wasn't sure. He looked like a sad puppy, afraid he'd done something wrong. Sweat dripped from his temples. His fever had climbed above 102; anything more than 100.5 is a huge concern for a cancer patient.

The resident ordered an emergency head scan. I didn't dare ask why. A stroke? Bleeding in his brain? Had the cancer spread there too?

"Does he have a Do Not Resuscitate order?" the resident asked apologetically.

Oh please, you have to ask me that, again, now? I mumbled something about how Elliot would want him to do what he could if there was a chance he'd recover enough to have a meaningful life. A vague answer to an impossible question.

At nearly midnight we went back down in the elevator to get the head scan. Waiting in the wheelchair, Elliot's jaw grew slack, his eyes vacant. He said nothing. I warned the technician that Elliot panicked in closed MRI machines, but it didn't matter this time. He was too dazed to notice.

What if something irreversible had happened? What if we'd gotten to a new place of permanent dementia? I'd handled a lot—his crazy diet, oozy dressings, relentless stress—but this I couldn't take: the prospect of nursing a husband who didn't know me. I could cope if I was in the thick of it with Elliot. Please don't make me go it alone. I need to be able to talk to my husband. He needs to talk to me too.

Once he was wheeled to the room, a patient aide tried to get him to lie down. Elliot stood stubbornly facing the bed in his light blue hospital gown, his hands on the mattress, refusing to budge. The aide looked at me like I should be able to manage my husband. I looked at her, hoping she knew what to do with out-of-control men. Then came what he would have horrified Elliot most—and I hate to say it—but he peed on the floor.

I pulled down his wet underwear. Suddenly there were three or four of us trying to cajole him into bed. It took us almost fifteen minutes to get him to turn around and bend his knees. He sat on the edge of the mattress like Rodin's *Thinker*. We tried to get him to lie down so he wouldn't fall.

"Just give me a minute," he complained suddenly, cranky and frayed. Thank God he was talking again. Tylenol had broken his fever and he drifted slowly back to reality. Eventually he lay down and slept.

The next morning Elliot had no memory of this entire episode. His thinking was as clear as ever. He was hungry and wanted *The Times*.

I told him vaguely what happened, but I didn't confess my fear he'd lost his mind forever. We had always told each other pretty much everything. Now I was piling up secrets because I didn't want to give him even more to worry about.

When the cluster of doctors and students crowded into the room on their daily rounds, I asked about the brain scan.

"It's negative," the resident announced.

"Brain scan's negative?" Elliot replied. "Guess nothing's there. No brain."

I burst out laughing with giddy relief. He was back.

LOOKING OVER THE ABYSS
November 2008

After five days in the hospital, we went home. Then Elliot spiked another fever and we bounced back to the hospital for a few more.

The weekend after his discharge we snuck off to Lambertville, pretending that he'd beaten back these raging infections for good. We napped all afternoon in a bed and breakfast so that he could handle a night out at one of our favorite restaurants. I put on a black leather skirt and black high heels. Obama had just won the election—I had wondered if Elliot would live to see that remarkable day—and everyone at Hamilton's Grill was abuzz with the news. Elliot fell asleep at the table after two bites of steak. The waiters must have thought me a very boring date.

After waffles the next morning, we stayed in bed until 2:00 p.m. What a luxury. We took a slow stroll through town, ending up back at the Phoenix bookstore, where I'd first thumbed through that *50 Essential Things to Do...* book on cancer. This was the only time we went to Lambertville without seeing the river. It was just too far to walk.

Three days later I was racing Elliot back to the hospital with another fever and another three days stuck on the sixteenth floor.

"Back again?" the nurses asked. Their eyes were full of sympathy and a sense of where we were headed. We knew all their names by now. Hope we get Daniella, we'd say grimly on the way in.

We had developed a routine at Sloan-Kettering – we'd stayed there for weeks if you totaled up the trips. I would call Elliot's mother and kids to update them. After the doctors made their morning rounds and Elliot started to nap, I'd check my laptop for work emails, tell my wonderfully flexible boss that I needed more time off, and then arrange carpools for Devon and Alex. I tried to treat the hospital like an alternate reality cruise ship. I had learned where to sneak off for a yoga class at the integrative medicine center or even a massage. I'd import minestrone and pasta with pesto from the Italian restaurant down the block, and sometimes invite friends to join us. Kate was great about visiting after work.

My favorite place in the hospital was the arts and recreation room. It was large and sunny with panoramic views of the vast city outside. It had a library, a piano, a pool table and closets full of games, puzzles and craft supplies. Elliot, his mother and I took a flower arranging class and made mosaics. I sewed a veritable zoo of stuffed animals made of felt. I came to know the weekly schedule for special projects by heart. Once when a doctor scheduled a procedure for 10:30 Tuesday morning, I couldn't help thinking "Oh no, we'll miss copper enameling."

Of course we had another chance on another trip. Elliot made me a seagull pendant in ocean greens. He was so drugged up, it was excruciating to watch him struggle to sprinkle the enamel powders onto the small piece of copper. He moved in slow motion and almost always missed the target. His whole body swayed with the effort. I treasure that necklace.

Elliot was discharged on Saturday, November 15. Not for long. At 4:30 Sunday morning, I woke up and felt his skin broil. No matter how much I pleaded, Elliot refused to get in the car.

"I will not go to that hospital," he insisted.

"He won't come with me," I cried to the on-call doctor. "Can we wait until it's light out?"

The doctor said okay but warned me to keep a close eye on him. Tylenol brought down his fever by 7:00 a.m., so Elliot felt vindicated. The next on-call doctor gave him permission to stay home and see how the day went. I wasn't so sure but felt outvoted.

Kate and Anthony were supposed to come to dinner. I asked her to bring some clothes just in case I needed her to spend the night with the kids. I made one of our favorites, penne with sautéed shrimp, sun-dried tomatoes and arugula. Just before dinner I felt Elliot's forehead. Hot again.

102.5.

As soon as Kate walked in the front door I told her I had to take Elliot to the city, right away. I gave him Tylenol to prevent delirium, kissed the kids goodnight and started another NASCAR dash over the George Washington Bridge.

In the car I fumed. I kicked myself I didn't force Elliot to come in earlier because whatever was wrong probably got worse during the day, though I suspected by this point it didn't matter anymore. Things seemed to be going inexorably downhill.

Back in the emergency room, Elliot sat on a gurney in the corner, staring miserably into space, elbow on his knee, chin on his hand, that damn paper ID bracelet back on his wrist. The admitting process always took forever. We were hungry but the hospital cafeteria was closed. I marched off to get cranberry juice from a free dispenser, getting more and more worked up as I filled the Styrofoam cup at the machine I'd been to a hundred times. He should have listened to me when I wanted to come in twelve hours ago. I stomped back down the hallway and sank down on top of a chair piled with our coats that was right next to Elliot's gurney.

"Tell me you're sorry and you love me," I demanded. "If I'm going to be responsible for taking care of you, you have to trust my judgment. This isn't fair to me."

"I'm sorry and I love you," he said obediently. Fat tears rolled down his face. He tried to wipe his eyes without taking off his glasses. He was too weary to move them. He looked unforgettably forlorn, his face wet and his body crumpled. I couldn't remember ever seeing him cry—except once before we were married when he thought we might break up.

"Don't you realize if I come in here again I'm not coming back out?"

That hit my gut like an iron mallet. At one of his lowest moments I'd gotten mad and made him feel worse. I jumped over to sit next to him, put both my arms around him and kissed his lips and face and neck.

"Oh Sweetie, I'm so sorry, I didn't mean to make you cry," I said. I was crying too. "I love you so much."

As heart-wrenching as it was to see him so hopeless, in such utter anguish, it also felt real. We sat there, my arms around him, our own island on the edge of a bustling emergency room, and together we mourned what our life had become. We were grieving, abandoning the let's-make-the-best-of-it stoicism, and if I could be glad for anything, it was for that feeling of truth between us. We could not have felt closer, and for that I was grateful. It would be too hard to peer over this abyss alone.

The next day, Monday, we were sitting on Elliot's bed. I was trying to finish something for work on my laptop. He looked at me, his deep brown eyes so wistful.

"It means so much to me to be married to you," he said. "I've been thinking a lot about our wedding vows, in sickness and in health. I try to live by them. I wish we'd had a ceremony that was more solemn. We've had such great times, I want more of them. I want to make love to you, take you to Paris, the south of France, Greece. I just don't know what is reasonable to hope for any more."

"I love you, Sweetie," I said. "Do you want to take a walk?"

"No, that's okay. I'll go. You do your work."

And he hobbled off with his IV pole to try to build up his strength. And I wrote down what he had just said. I wanted to keep his words safe.

Elliot was dozing on Tuesday afternoon. I was sitting at his feet on his bed, knitting another scarf that would never be worn. Helen was reading in a chair by the door. Dr. Kelsen walked in. As usual, his thin face looked formal, sober and inscrutable behind his wire-rimmed glasses.

"So what's really happening here?" I asked on an impulse,

grabbing a rare chance to talk to the doctor who knew Elliot best. We had heard only details about blood tests and antibiotics from the others. We hadn't heard anything about the big picture. I usually didn't ask for the grand view, because I was reluctant to elicit more information than Elliot wanted. At this point, though, I needed to know.

"What should we expect?"

"Let's step outside," Dr. Kelsen said.

I turned to my mother-in-law. "Helen, do you want to hear this? Or maybe not?"

She pushed herself out of the chair. We went into the hallway, a public space for the most private of conversations. I leaned against the wall and held Helen close to my side with my hand against her back, rubbing it slowly up and down, to catch her if she fainted.

"He's very ill," the doctor said. "Very, very ill. He's been very ill for three months."

I tried to think straight, tried to figure out what I really needed to ask.

"So are you telling me I should call his kids to come?"

"If you absolutely want to guarantee that they see him again, yes."

Perhaps his urgent tone shouldn't have come as a surprise. But the other doctors seemed to be treating this—Elliot's fourth hospital stay in a month—as just another infection. Nobody had let on that deep inside his body, things had gotten so much worse. Or maybe I just wasn't hearing them.

"How much time do we have?" I asked.

"It could be any day, or any hour"

I sucked in my breath.

"Or it could be a week or two. We really don't know."

"What do I tell them?"

"They know he has cancer, don't they?"

"Of course. But he was doing so well for so long."

"You can tell them I think it's a good idea for them to come see him."

Helen, who had been trying to absorb all this in stricken silence, spoke now.

"This is such a crime," she said, shaking her head in dismay at a world that would do this to her son. "He was just telling me he loves his life. He loves his wife. He loves his job."

"I'm sorry," the doctor said somberly. "It's a very difficult disease."

"I don't think Elliot understands what's happening," I said. "I think he's in denial. Should we tell him?"

"I would never strip a man of his defenses."

I couldn't let myself feel what all this really meant. I couldn't afford to collapse. I had to take care of everybody. I had to manage the kids. But if we had come to some kind of endpoint, it seemed to me that we should tell Dr. Kelsen that we didn't blame him. Elliot's trust in his doctor helped him stay strong, and Elliot would want to show his appreciation. I thought I should speak for him.

"Thank you." My voice cracked. "We know you did your best."

That didn't seem sufficient. So I looked at this reserved and formidable doctor, a man so exacting that he routinely made med students quake, and threw my arms around him in a tight hug. He was taken aback but submitted. Despite his waste-no-time, intimidating demeanor, this man was deeply humane.

So I made those dreaded urgent phone calls, and Kate came right up on the subway from Soho. Her face was wet, red and puffy. I had never seen her cry before, just that knuckle to the corner of her eye at our wedding. Elliot was dozing, and I got up from my spot at his side and asked if she wanted a turn there for a while. When she lay down on that rumpled bed alongside her father, I thought her grandmother's heart would crack open.

Max jumped on a bus from Ithaca. Aaron flew in from Chicago. Their mother, eager to help, brought them to the hospital. They arrived at 1:30 in the morning.

Elliot was awake and heard their voices outside in the hall. He turned to me. "I thought you'd pull off a stunt like this," he said with a big smile.

He thought it was some kind of surprise party to cheer him up. He didn't seem to realize it was all about guaranteeing a chance to say goodbye.

I heard him tell friends about it later, how Max and Aaron snuck into the hospital in the middle of the night, like it was some kind of whimsical caper. He described it with a certain glee.

The next morning, Devon and Alex skipped school to visit. Their dad kindly brought them in. When I met my kids in the lobby and they saw my face, their eyes grew wide. I told them Elliot might come home, but he might not, and if there was anything they wanted to tell him, this would be a good time. We all cried, and we hugged, and then we got ourselves together to march to the elevator and head upstairs.

After a lunch of take-out sandwiches and the welcome diversion of a pet therapy visit from a giant bull mastiff named Lily, all the kids sat with Elliot and his mother and me at a big round table making things in the sunny art room. Alex made him a mosaic that said "Let's Go Mets." Devon wove him a bracelet out of embroidery thread. Kate sewed him a stuffed dragon. Max and Aaron made jokes. I marveled that we could actually be having a good time together when Elliot was so terribly sick. Even then, his ability to find pleasure in things, especially in our family, was a life-giving force.

HOME

To my surprise—actually, alarm—a day after all the kids came to visit Sloan-Kettering, Elliot was discharged. His chart said his condition was "poor." So why send him away? The only treatment they could give him was a mix of high-octane antibiotics, and that could be done at home. By me.

We had reached some kind of serious crossroads but nobody at the hospital brought up the idea of hospice. That was not only baffling, it was hurtful. I needed experienced help, and the medical staff should have made it easier for me to say so, especially when Elliot would never acknowledge hospice as the next step. Apparently doctors don't like to admit defeat either.

A case manager started to arrange for a visiting nurse and a high-tech nurse who would teach me how to do a complicated type of home IV.

"I need more help," I said. "Do you think we should get hospice?"

"That is one option," the case manager said, not very usefully.

"I think we need to try it. I've heard some people regret it when they wait too long. If he gets better we can cancel it, right?"

"Yes. I'll ask the doctor to write the order."

I was losing my grip, everything seemed to be happening so fast. I told Elliot I was signing up for an agency that would give us more help. He would be shaken by the H-word. To get hospice care, a doctor has to confirm that a patient has less than six months to live. This was a truly dire step, but I needed backup. I didn't see it as giving up but as recruiting more hands to manage the inevitable. After more than two years of weekly or biweekly chemo trips, then radiation, and nine emergency hospital stays, including four in the past month, I was wrung out. Drained. Out of gas. Just when my responsibilities at home were mounting astronomically. And this had to be my decision. Doctors had already asked me to sign an updated Do Not Resuscitate order. By calling on me as Elliot's health care proxy, they were signaling they thought he was no longer coherent enough to make choices on his own.

A high-tech nurse, a dedicated woman from a different agency than the hospice company, came to teach me how to give Elliot an IV antibiotic called Invanz. You had to mix the chemicals with sterile technique, keeping all the various pieces clean with alcohol wipes at every step. You had to be an octopus to hold all the pieces. The fifteen-step instruction sheet took a full page, single-spaced. It was full of intimidating warnings in capital letters, like REMEMBER TO KEEP THE NEEDLE BELOW THE LEVEL OF THE FLUID! And DO NOT TOUCH SPIKE!

There were so many opportunities to screw up. During my practice session I felt my face flush hot. After dissolving the medicine I couldn't suck it back into the syringe properly. I needed multiple do-overs. Then I couldn't get the IV flow adjusted to the ideal speed of six drops per fifteen seconds. It kept going too fast or too slow. I felt the sting behind my eyes that told me tears were coming.

"You're overwhelmed," the nurse said. "But this IV isn't what's overwhelming you. It's the whole situation. You can do this. Take a deep breath."

After a few days I got the hang of it. I don't know how anyone with poor language skills, a disorganized life or a dirty house could handle it.

The hospice people started coming by. I thought they would make things easier. I was dead wrong. The case manager had recommended an agency that turned out to be a farce. We were supposed to get one steady nurse who would get to know us. Didn't happen. One lady arrived at our house reeking of cigarette smoke. It was hard to take medical advice from her. She didn't do much anyway, just stopped by for fifteen minutes, took Elliot's blood pressure and filled out paperwork. The next nurse kept arriving late. Another simply didn't show up. A physical therapist kept postponing and never came at all.

Hospice has an angelic glow, a reputation for helping people die with dignity, without all the painful tubes and grueling interventions that ultimately do no good. In our case, hospice was like lemon juice on a raw wound. The only helpful thing the company did was arrange deliveries of medical equipment—an oxygen machine, a walker, a shower chair. No doubt there are wonderful hospices out there. This one was just a profitable system for reimbursement. During the deepest crisis of my life, I felt cruelly ripped off. I berated myself for signing up with this company, but there was no time to find a better one.

Ironically, Elliot, the one in a methadone fog, saw through them right away.

"Who are these people?" he asked me one morning, his words slurring. "What's their business model?"

"Honey, I just need some more help around here."

I started my days crying silently in bed before dawn, before anyone could hear me. I tried to savor my husband's skin against mine, to etch the feeling in my mind. How long, I wondered, will I wake up next to him? How long can we limp along like this? Who will fall apart first, Elliot or me?

Then I would dry my face, get up to count out his seventeen pills, help him get down the stairs, cook him breakfast, drive the kids to school, help him shower and wrestle clean socks onto his strangely swollen feet. By the time I got him cleaned up I was sweating and exhausted. And it was only 10:00 a.m.

The real help came from our family.

Elliot's mother, who hated to sleep anywhere but her own bed, couldn't bear to be away from him, so she moved in to Max's old Star Wars crash pad in the attic. Helen busied herself cleaning. She needed something to do with her hands. My house has never been so spic-and-span. Elliot's sister Marjorie flew in from England. It was almost Thanksgiving, so Max and Aaron didn't go back to college or Chicago after their dramatic middle-of-the-night appearance at the hospital. They camped out at our house too. Backpacks, laptops and cell phone chargers spontaneously generated all over the living room, along with sleeping bags and pillows for the couch and a cot. They did errands, picked up milk and brought home bagels. Devon and Alex, who were on Thanksgiving break too, helped with the dishes. Kate and her boyfriend came by all the time. Aaron's girlfriend, Sallie, joined us.

Overnight, it seemed, our home had become a hotel and mini-hospital. With eight to eleven of us around at any time, mountains of groceries came in. Mountains of garbage went out. The older kids took turns making dinner. Aaron made stir-fried chicken and broccoli for everyone; Kate made baked fish with spinach.

I was touched to see how much they wanted to help me as well as their dad. It had occurred to me in the past that if their father was gone their connection to me might fade away. But they were being so supportive and thoughtful, I came to have faith that their tie to me and my kids would last even after their father's presence no longer bound them to us.

Everyone pitched in. Their mother brought over two huge pans of lasagna and two apple pies with a cheery mid-Western smile.

"I know how my group eats," Janet said.

Friends dropped by at a moment's notice to say hi and entertain us, adding to a communal feeling of warmth. Nobody fussed over table manners, nobody put out fancy glasses for company. We burned through tons of paper plates.

After I got my private pre-dawn tears out of my system, those days were remarkably rich. Elliot smiled as he dozed on the couch, listening to the hubbub of having us all around, fussing over him. We watched movies and took walks. Everybody teased me as I sat at the dining room table, finishing a goofy centerpiece I started in the Sloan-Kettering art room using paper maché, crumpled newspapers and gold spray paint. It was a turkey. I made a pilgrim's hat out of black construction paper and glued it on his head at a jaunty angle. Elliot loved it, as I knew he would.

"That's my girl," he said with a chuckle.

When we could ignore the backdrop, we could actually have some fun.

Nobody used the word "hospice."

So much was left unsaid, yet as a family we had never felt closer.

One day I was out getting provisions when Elliot felt a little burst of energy and hatched a plan. He craved a slice from Brooklyn Pizza, a Hackensack joint he loved taking his kids to when they were little. He hadn't had pizza in two years. The girls were busy and out of the house. This would be an adventure for the guys.

It took until 5:00 p.m. for Aaron to help Elliot get showered and dressed. Alex and Max waited patiently but hoped to get out the door before I came home. They thought I'd say no, the expedition was too risky, like I was some kind of Nurse Ratched from *One Flew Over the Cuckoo's Nest*. Their presumption of my disapproval made the whole scheme that much more delicious.

I got home just as they were leaving.

"We're going for pizza," Elliot announced. "I'm just going to have one slice."

"Okay" I said, surprised. "Be careful. Don't forget your medicine."

Alex had his hands in his pockets, trying to look nonchalant, but it was clear he was excited to be heading off on a mission with the men.

I acted concerned so they could relish their rebelliousness, but in truth, I couldn't have been happier with their prison break. If Elliot could get such a thrill from a simple piece of pizza with our boys, that was a beautiful thing.

I wanted them to have these moments to remember. These seemed to be our last chances. Elliot seemed to be slipping away.

One day, he was sitting at the dining room table, hunched over a small lined notebook, writing painstakingly in capital letters.

"TO WHOM IT MAY" he wrote on the top of one page.

"TO WHOM IT" he wrote on top of the next page. Every time he thought he'd made a mistake, he moved to another page, another try.

TO W

TO WHOM IT MAY CONCERN

TO WHO

He went on for several more pages. Was this some kind of will?

"What are you doing?" I asked softly.

He looked perturbed. "I'm not really sure."

"Okay," I said, squeezing his shoulder. And we left it at that.

Another day I found him staring at his computer for hours, thinking he was working. Only a few random letters were typed on the screen. Doctors said this confusion might come from a lack of oxygen, a buildup of drugs, and the accumulation of toxins in his blood due to his weakening liver. Unsettling incidents often revolved around food. He looked at his cereal bowl at breakfast one morning and thought it was a steaming bowl of meat and vegetables. Another day he thought his oxygen machine was feeding him his favorite soup from the Italian restaurant nearby.

"Where's the ribollita?" he asked, disconcerted. I said there wasn't any.

"I must be losing my mind," he said. He looked disappointed in himself.

I knew things were really bad one evening when he was watching TV. His show ended and *Alvin and the Chipmunks* came on. Those squeaky sing-song cartoon voices were so nasal and annoying. Even though Elliot was holding the remote, he didn't change the channel.

His legs were so heavy with swelling he couldn't move easily in bed at night. He nodded and put out his hands to let me know he wanted to spoon. So I pulled him onto his side, stacking his right leg onto his left, and then nestled into his side to get in position.

I couldn't bear the thought he might reach a place where he didn't seem to love me anymore. I wrote myself a note for the day I would need reassurance.

"He uses oxygen more and more—all evening watching TV after dinner," I typed in an email to myself. "But he still says I love you back every time I say I love you. He still puts his hand on my ass to take a nap. Even when he seems asleep, if I kiss him he kisses back, or if I say I love you he kisses the air. I have to keep remembering he loves me in case there's a time he can't show it so well."

I charted his affection the way nurses chart vital signs. I had to document what mattered.

THANKSGIVING
2008

"Do you think this year we could maybe have just one Thanksgiving?" Kate asked one night while we were doing dishes. Usually she went to her mom's house with her brothers for one holiday meal, and then came to our house for another.

"That's fine with me, but we should poll the troops," I said. Everyone agreed. Ease ruled.

I made turkey, corn bread stuffing, mashed potatoes and salad. Janet brought over casseroles: one with sweet potatoes and marshmallows, one with string beans, onions and almonds.

We decided to start the festivities around 5:00 to take advantage of Elliot's most alert phase of the day. About an hour and a half beforehand I began helping him shower and get dressed. He wore sweatpants and a loose black fleece with a little Mets logo that Alex had given him years ago. Now it was useful for hiding his swollen belly. It took ages to work the socks up over his feet. They were as round as bear paws. His new size twelve slippers hardly fit. I held Elliot's arm as he trudged slowly, step by step, down the stairs. He leaned so hard on the banister I was afraid it might break.

I set the table for twelve with the maroon tablecloth that I brought out for special occasions. I'd always loved that tablecloth. My mother had made it out of a patterned print from India when I was little and passed it on to me. It had some rips and fraying seams, but it gave me sentimental comfort.

Nobody said it, but we all sensed it would likely be our last holiday with Elliot. We hauled out the video camera. Devon shot a hectic scene as everyone carried out heaping platters, searched for serving spoons, decided who would go to the buffet first. The shot caught Elliot taking his place at the head of the table, wincing as he lowered himself down to his chair.

He looked so weary. His face was so thin you could see the lines of his skull. His cheeks were gaunt and sunken like that ghost in the Munsch painting, *The Scream*. There were deep circles under his eyes. His cheekbones were sharp.

"We're not, like, saying stuff?" Max asked.

"Sure, Max you start," I said. "Make a nice toast. It was your idea."

"I'm not good at stand-up."

"You don't have to stand up," said Elliot's sister Marjorie.

"I mean improv, or whatever you call it. But okay," Max paused. "Yeah, well…We're all here."

There was nervous laughter.

"May I?" asked Aaron, ever the older brother, showing he thought he could do it better. I couldn't help rushing to Max's defense. The fact that Elliot didn't do so himself showed he was in a daze.

"Wait," I said. "Max got very much to the point. That's exactly it. We're all here is a really profound thing to say."

"Our glasses to that," Max's mother said to back me up. We held our glasses high and took a sip.

I told Aaron he could have a turn. He took on a master-of-ceremonies formality.

"I'd just like to thank everyone for being here," he said with an endearing bit of pomp, "and for working together to make this really great dinner, so we could all be together, really all of us, the entire family here now."

"'Look, now he's the boss," his aunt Marjorie teased.

"Oh come on," Aaron continued. "As a family, a somewhat extended family, we get together so infrequently it's great to have everyone sitting around the table tonight.'

I took another quick video shot of everyone digging in but didn't

174

want to film too long. I didn't want to seem too conspicuous about saving the moment for the future.

Afterwards we all sat around the fire playing one of our favorite games, "Twenty-five words or less." You got a card naming five nouns, celebrities, places or works of art. You had to use pithy clues—twenty-five words at the most—to get your team to say all five words on the card within sixty seconds.

The kids were competitive. Alex, who was good at this despite being the youngest, wanted to trade Marjorie off our team. As always, Kate and I were on the same wavelength to an uncanny degree. Elliot tried to keep up, but it was difficult so he was quiet. Still, he smiled with fatherly pride at all the antics around him.

"A prickly animal," Janet prompted.

"A hedgehog," Kate said. "Porcupine."

"Yes!"

Soon it was Kate's turn to give clues.

"Build a better…"

"Mousetrap!" Elliot answered.

"Yes!" We all beamed. He was back in the game.

His turn to give clues, however, was a challenge. He forgot that you had to use as few words as possible. He chattered on and on. "This is something you could try to eat but that would be highly unlikely," he said.

Alex looked at me and I looked at Devon, the scorekeeper. She had the sensitivity to stop counting his words—he had far exceeded his limit. She hid the hourglass under the table and we all humored him, bending the rules the way we would for a child.

Kate made a fantastic spread for dessert. Chocolate tarts with strawberries on top in a walnut crust. Homemade walnut pepper ice cream. Chocolate port ice cream. Coffee gelato with chocolate-covered coffee beans. Pumpkin bread pudding.

175

Devon must have picked up the camera. The video shows us all passing plates and digging in. Elliot's head is drooping, almost on to the table. I'm standing by his chair and lean over to put my arms around him.

"Oh, Sweetie's so tired," I say quietly. It sounds like I'm soothing a baby.

9-1-1

After Thanksgiving, Elliot seemed stable, like he'd reached a plateau, so Elliot's kids and sister went back home. It was up to me and Helen to look after him. We thought he was safe in his green armchair.

He loved that chair. It was ugly as sin, a hand-me-down covered in fake velvet with olive and gold stripes, but it was incredibly comfortable. It took up an inviting spot by our bedroom window.

I had no clue how hard it had become for Elliot to push himself out of its soft, deep cushions.

Then late one night, I was stealing a few minutes of peace in front of the TV downstairs when I heard a giant crash above me. I raced upstairs. Elliot lay face down on the floor. He had tried get out of the chair but fallen straight over, like a tree in the cartoons when a logger yells "timber." The round coffee table had broken his fall and the impact had split off a wooden leg. The tabletop lay beside him like a slanted moon. Magazines were scattered everywhere. Luckily an empty water glass hadn't shattered. Elliot looked humiliated lying immobile in the mess. His jaw was clenched.

It took every ounce of my strength to reposition his leaden legs and swivel him around to face the heavy chair. It took every ounce of his to hoist himself up on it by his arms. We didn't say much about the accident. I just kissed him.

A few days later, he was back in the chair.

"So this is what it means to 'succumb to the complications of cancer'," he said, quoting the obituary cliché.

"Oh, Sweetie," I said. I kneeled on the floor, put my head in his lap and put my arms around him. "I love you."

I didn't want to say "you'll beat this" or "we'll get through this," or anything patently false. I didn't want lies between us.

"I'm here with you" was all I could think to say.

I just couldn't bear to confine him upstairs in that chair, or in bed, like an invalid. That would surely sink him into the deepest depression. But it was becoming harder for him to get around.

One night Elliot wanted to change the TV station. The remote was broken and I was upstairs, so he got down on all fours to try to push the channel button. Then he couldn't lift himself back on the couch. I couldn't pull him up either. Helen's face fell.

I dialed 9-1-1.

"Hi, this is Leslie Brody," I told the dispatcher. "It's not an emergency, but my husband is sick and got on the floor and I can't get him up. Can you please send over two strong men?"

"Is he in any pain?"

"No, he's okay, he just can't get up."

Within minutes a volunteer ambulance unit arrived, Siren screaming.

"How are you doing Sir?" one of the men asked kindly.

"I'm okay," Elliot said. "I'm just stuck."

"Are you in any pain?"

"No. I just got down here like a schmuck and can't get up again."

One said don't worry, they did this all the time. It's called a lift-assist. Who knew?

The two men linked arms behind Elliot's back, under his armpits, and in one deft motion they hoisted him up straight. They escorted him to a chair at the dining table. Elliot accepted their help so humbly it was touching. I could see a lesser man fuming.

"You're looking a little jaundiced, Sir," one volunteer said, checking his vitals. I had gotten so used to Elliot's yellow complexion I barely noticed anymore.

"Yeah, well, it's been that way for a while," he said. "It's okay."

"He has pancreatic cancer," I added.

"Ah, I see. Well, take care, Sir. If you need us again, don't hesitate."

As soon as they left I put a fifty dollar check in the mail to the volunteer ambulance corps. I thought back in shame over all the times I'd thrown their fundraising letters into the trash.

I was a wreck. I was also trying to spend some time with Alex after he got home from school. I'd been so consumed with Elliot, I was afraid Alex was feeling neglected. Every single time I sat down on the couch to hear about Alex's day at school, or sign his homework, or watch a bit of baseball with him, Helen kept butting in.

"Elliot says he needs his pain medicine," she said.

"Okay, fine, just a minute, I'll get it."

Then a little later, "Elliot's still sleeping," she said. "It's been a long time."

"It's okay. Let him rest."

Then a little later, "Elliot wants some of that strawberry milk. I don't know where it is. Can you make some?"

"Sure."

Alex rolled his eyes. He was polite to Helen but getting sick of the interruptions too. He grumbled when I said I better get started on dinner, maybe he could hang in the kitchen with me? I put pasta on to boil. I didn't have the energy for anything else.

Of course that's when Elliot called me because he needed to go upstairs to the bathroom. Alas, we didn't have one on the first floor. I hadn't ordered one of those humiliating portable "commodes" because I just couldn't see Elliot ever agreeing to use one.

So he began the trudge upstairs. We had a method. I crouched behind him, my head by his legs. As he swung his left foot back off a step, I'd catch it and push it up onto the next step. Then he swung his right foot back, I'd catch it and hoist it to the next step. He leaned so hard on the banister I was afraid it would break.

Elliot dragged himself up, step by tedious step, until he got to the landing. It took almost twenty minutes.

"I have to sit," he gasped. "I'm out of gas."

He was stuck.

So I dialed 9-1-1 again. I couldn't believe we needed another hand so soon, just two days after our last call. Within minutes a young policeman built like a football player was at our door. He had a shiny black gun in his holster. Alex's eyes grew wide as he came to see, then he backed away to play at the computer. Maybe he was timid. Maybe he didn't want to seem morbidly curious, like a rubbernecker at a car crash.

The policeman bolted up the stairs. Elliot was slumped against a wall, his legs stuck straight out in front of him like a rag doll in sweat pants.

"Hello, Sir. How are you?"

"Okay, I just couldn't go any further."

In one big heave he got Elliot to his feet.

"Where do you want to go Sir?"

"The green chair over there."

"Sweetie," I intervened. "Don't you think you might want to get in bed?" I dreaded having to call 9-1-1 a third time just to get him up from the chair.

"No, I want to go to the chair."

Mr. Stubborn.

I went downstairs and made a different kind of emergency call. To Aaron.

"Hi, it's Leslie. I'm sorry, I don't want to scare you, but I need your muscle here."

"Is he alright?"

"Well, he's having a harder time getting around. Especially with the stairs."

180

"I could get a flight tomorrow or Sunday."

"How about tomorrow. Please."

By this time it was 8:30 p.m.

Helen came downstairs, her forehead furrowed.

"Leslie, Alex hasn't had dinner yet. Don't you think he should eat?"

"Helen, I've been a little busy. I'm getting there."

I rushed around the kitchen, throwing red sauce into a pot to heat. I'd boiled the pasta before the police came. It was cold and hard and dried out. I put a bowl of it with butter and a little water in the microwave to warm up for Alex.

As I spooned red sauce on three bowls of pasta for the rest of us – as if Elliot would eat some – Helen walked in.

"But Leslie," she said. "Alex doesn't like sauce."

That did it.

"Helen, I know my own son," I snapped. I grabbed her face in my hands, one hand on each cheek, shoved my face up close to hers and glowered into her eyes.

"LET ME DO MY DAMN JOB. I am spending all my time and energy taking care of your son. Give me a MINUTE to take care of mine."

The microwave beeped and I threw the pasta for Alex on the table. It was still hard and dry but I couldn't manage dealing with one more problem. None of us ate anyway.

In the morning I apologized. Helen waved her hands to shoo the incident away. She understood I was at wit's end and I didn't mean to be so harsh. She had been through something like this herself years ago. I admired how she was taking all this in and letting me be in charge. If my child were dying, I'd have an awfully hard time just helping from the sidelines. I'd want to be first in command.

My husband was sitting in that green chair again when he uttered the last slow, lucid words that were meant just for me.

"You. Are. So. Great." He shook his head in what looked like regret. I imagine he was thinking of all the things he knew he would miss.

"I love you too, Sweetie."

On Saturday Elliot spent hours dozing in that green chair. We all silently accepted he couldn't manage the stairs. As we waited for Aaron to arrive from Chicago, Alex rigged up a DVD player so Elliot could watch the Mets game and *WALL-E* in our bedroom. He didn't have the attention span to focus much anyway. When Alex noticed that Elliot had trouble drinking from a glass, he ran to the kitchen to get straws. He was so eager to try to help.

"This is it," Elliot mumbled. He seemed so far away. "This is the day."

His mother said later that sometimes people knew. I don't know how.

That green chair was where Elliot ate his last meal, as Aaron and Kate tried to coax down a few bites of apple pie.

That was where Kate tried to brush her father's teeth.

That was where I would one day find a half-bitten, red-and-white medicine capsule under the seat cushion. It must have fallen out of his mouth. I saved it in a box, like it was an artifact, a fossil, a relic of another era.

We never really got to say goodbye. Maybe that was a mercy. Because, in the end, what would you say? How could you possibly bear it?

DRIFTING AWAY
December 13, 14 & 15

"I want my fucking medicine!" he cried out on that infernal Saturday night.

"It's not time yet," I said, as if keeping a schedule still mattered.

"I want it now!" he shouted, glaring. Those were his last clear words.

Belligerence could be part of the final stages, the glossy hospice brochure had said.

"Okay. But then you'll have to wait a while to have more."

And so the end began. I tried desperately to get him comfortable. Put a pillow behind his back. Got him water. Helped him get up. Helped him lie down. Woke up my stepson to help carry Elliot to the bathroom. Called the hospice for advice. He wasn't making sense.

Give him Haldol, the nurse said.

Does that conflict with his Zyprexa? I asked.

I'm not sure, give him Ativan and I'll get back to you, she said.

She didn't call back.

I should have called Sloan-Kettering. It was hours after midnight and I wasn't thinking straight.

I called the hospice back. Give him more Ativan, she said.

He got worse, restless and wild-eyed, babbling incoherently.

Terminal agitation, the brochure said.

Part of me didn't think this was really it. Not yet. There had been so many setbacks before, and he had come back. Maybe this would go on for days. Part of me knew. He kept lurching forward, acting like he wanted to sit up, so I pulled him up by the arms and stuffed a pillow behind his back. Again and again. There were six pillows behind him. Seven. Not enough. I ran to the hallway closet to find more. His feet dangled off the end of the bed.

I woke Aaron again for more help, then called the hospice back.

Can you send someone to tell us what to do? I asked.

The nurse can come first thing in the morning, she said.

But that's hours away.

It doesn't sound urgent, she said.

Fucking bitch.

By 8:00 a.m. Sunday, the nurse still hadn't come.

I hadn't slept all night.

I called the hospice again. I wished I'd called Sloan-Kettering.

Brenda will be at your house in forty-five minutes, she said.

That nurse took one look at Elliot and said, "He needs to go to our inpatient unit. He doesn't know where he is. They will stabilize him. Then he can come home."

That was a lie. I knew it. She knew I knew.

She called an ambulance.

I called Milo to come get Devon and Alex. They were too young for this.

"Sweetie," I said to Devon. "We need to take Elliot to the agency's inpatient place. Would you like to say anything to him? Maybe tell him to feel better?"

She swallowed hard, nodded yes. She came with me to my room. Elliot was lying back, quieter now, spent, silent. His eyes narrowed. He looked at her.

"Feel better, Elliot," she said. Tears fell down her face. She tugged at her hair. "We'll see you when you get home."

He didn't answer. She knew what was happening.

I hugged her.

"You did a beautiful job," I said. "I'm sure it means a lot to him."

Alex was downstairs at the computer.

"Would you like to say 'feel better' to Elliot?" I asked. I didn't want my son to be haunted if he didn't say goodbye.

Alex shook his head no. Kept staring at the screen. So scared.

Milo picked up the kids.

The ambulance came.

They wrapped Elliot in a sheet like a straitjacket so he wouldn't flail his arms and hurt himself when they carried him down the stairs.

They strapped him into a stretcher, shoved him in the back of the ambulance.

I climbed in back with him. So did his mother. Aaron would follow in a cab with Kate.

It was freezing cold.

They didn't have a blanket.

Assholes. How could they not have blankets in an ambulance?

Elliot didn't even seem to notice. He was murmuring gibberish.

I kissed him but he didn't kiss back.

So I kissed him again and again.

Maybe this was his last gift, getting so delirious he had to be taken to the inpatient place. As much as I thought I could handle it if he died in our bedroom, that would have been creepy for the kids. He spared us that nightmare.

The inpatient place was dingy, despicable. The worn grey carpet, the token smattering of holiday tinsel, the slim window with a view of a dirty air shaft. The nurse didn't let me stay with Elliot when they got him settled into bed in a pale blue hospital gown. She combed his hair straight to the side, like a little boy's at the barber. As soon as I could join him I had to muss it, run my fingers through it, make it wave toward the back like usual.

Everybody tells you bearing a child can be agony. Nobody warns you about watching a man die. I assumed Elliot would simply slip away in his sleep. I couldn't have been more wrong.

Elliot's labored breaths were like groans. I strained to find the words in his chatter but couldn't decipher any syllables that made sense. He stared straight ahead. I kissed him. It was a one-way kiss.

Aaron and Kate came in a taxi. They put on the overhead TV and found a football game in hopes it would make Elliot feel more at home. It sounded tinny and irritating, but I didn't want to overrule them. In a vain attempt to make things feel normal at dinner time, they brought in Chinese take-out. I got down a few sips of wonton soup. The hours went by. Kate sat reading, holding Elliot's hand. I kissed his forehead, watched him, kissed him, cried.

I kept asking the nurse if he was really comfortable, he seemed to be grimacing. She said yes. I didn't believe her. Listening to his raspy moaning was pure torture.

When the night shift nurse came in, her eyes widened.

"It looks like he's in pain," she said.

I blew up.

"Your ONLY job is to make him comfortable," I hissed. "Can't you people do that ONE thing right?"

He'd had the best doctors in the world when he was sick. And now, in the very last stretch, these incompetents were screwing everything up. He had such a bad cancer. Didn't he deserve a good death? I loathed these people. I was disgusted with myself for not finding a better hospice, but there was so little time, and I really thought he would die in his sleep at home.

The new nurse upped the morphine, added some other drugs, and he seemed to relax, finally. At midnight Janet arrived with Max, who'd gotten on the first bus from Ithaca. She took Kate and Aaron home for a little sleep. I would let her stay with us when they returned. I understood she wanted to be with her children.

Helen and Max slept in chairs. I tried to squeeze in with Elliot, to sleep with him once more, but his bed was too narrow. There was no room for me. He was going someplace and I couldn't go with him.

At 5:00 a.m. I started writing, eleven tight pages, so many things I didn't want to forget. I would find later that the moron social worker had taken notes on me: "She seems more preoccupied with being a record-keeper than being with Elliot."

What the hell did he know? Not a damn thing. I had given my life to this man, been to every doctor's appointment, cleaned his bile and bruised my knees on the floor to bathe him like a baby. I had done everything I could. And now I was going to be left alone. And this imbecile of a social worker, with an insipid handlebar mustache, was judging me for writing? I wanted to remember everything. I wanted to save our lives, at least on paper.

And yet, in the face of such fury and anguish, there were moments of beauty.

When all of Elliot's kids were back Monday morning, we took turns sitting in the chair by his head, on his right. Nobody talked about taking turns, it just happened. His head was turned slightly to the side, and even though he wasn't moving, and his stare seemed vacant, that's the seat where you felt like you were with him the most. So I sat there for a while, then got up and asked Kate if she'd like a turn, and then after a while she gave up the seat for her grandmother and brothers. We just kept rotating around, in silent, sensitive generosity. That I will always remember, with pride.

It was all coming down to this. This was it, after so much time and care and effort. I had tried to stifle my tears, keep them under control, but I couldn't any more. I wept. Loud, keening sobs. Kate leaned over and hugged me. It was so sweet to find her wanting to reassure me. I had thought I had to be responsible for everyone else. And here she wanted to give some comfort to me.

At some point my mother called my cell phone. She knew things were getting worse and wondered if I needed help with my kids.

"I hate this place," I said as I sat in the hallway for a moment. "They under-medicated him and he was so agitated. I'm kicking myself that I didn't find a better hospice."

My mother's voice cracked as she spoke, word by careful word. "I. Will. Not. Let. You. Criticize. Yourself," she said. "You have done too well."

After all this time, more than two years of barely a comment about Elliot's illness or my struggle to take care of him, here she was telling me I had done a good job. I shook my head in disbelief and allowed myself a grain of satisfaction. My mother's praise let me grant myself a morsel of forgiveness.

Then my dad called. I talked to him from the hallway. "How am I going to do this?" I cried.

"I have total confidence in you," he said. I was glad to hear his voice, but didn't stay on the phone for long. I was afraid to be out of Elliot's room.

His breathing had become so quiet, so slow, it was hard to tell what was happening. He wasn't on any kind of monitor. That was a blessing. I've heard of families so transfixed by the beeping dot on the screen they lose track of the person they love. We all watched Elliot. You could see a subtle little bump of pulse beating slowly on his neck. That seemed the only clue. I kept staring at that one spot. And then it was still.

Aaron looked at me.

"Is that it?" he asked quietly.

"I don't know," I said. "I think so."

And we cried, and we looked at Elliot's face, trying to savor this last chance. Aaron put his hands near his father's eyes and gave me a questioning look.

"Should I?" he asked.

Yes, I guess so, I nodded. So Aaron passed his fingers down gently over his father's eyelids. But they wouldn't stay shut. Elliot had fought so hard, and it seemed like he still refused to leave us.

I didn't know how I would leave him either. He hated to be alone. But already tiny red blotches were blooming on his jaundiced skin, and his cheeks were falling slacker into his bones, and I was afraid if we stayed too long we might see his body change in ways we would regret.

So I gave my husband those final, final, final last kisses, all over his forehead and cheeks and even his dry papery lips.

"I love you, Sweetie," I whispered into his ear. "You saved my life."

THE PERFECT THING

I sat in a stupor in the taxi going home. Elliot's mother and Aaron came with me. We didn't talk. I felt nauseous.

Devon and Alex got home from school. They could read what happened in my face. I took them into the TV room to sit on the couch with me.

"Elliot's gone," I said.

"I'm so sorry, Mommy," Devon said through her tears.

We sat there, our arms around each other, crying. Then Aaron walked in.

"We're still a family," he said. "We love you guys."

What a perfect thing to say.

We hugged.

Then we dispersed to recover. Aaron, Kate and Max went to their mom's house. Elliot's mother wanted to be in her apartment alone.

That night my children took care of me.

Alex built a fire. Devon drew me a hot bath. They unplugged the phone. They put on music. They ordered sesame chicken. They poured me a glass of wine.

Somehow they knew exactly what to do.

THE FIRST DAYS

"Cremation," I told the man at the funeral home. It's not what Elliot wanted but this was the one gift I allowed myself. I simply could not bear to picture him underground, cold, alone in the dark. This was cleaner, natural, ashes to ashes.

"What would you like us to do with his wedding ring?" the man asked.

"Will the gold melt?" I asked. "If it doesn't melt and I sprinkle him in the wind, is there a chance the ring will fall into the mud?"

"It's possible."

"So how am I supposed to choose?" I wailed. I wanted his ring, our ring, to stay with him, to keep him company, but I didn't want its molten remains to land in the dirt at my feet.

Okay, I said. I'll keep it. Someone somewhere would have to ease it off his finger. I hated to think of such an intimate act being done by a stranger who didn't even care. I didn't even know where Elliot was at that very moment. I could not believe I would not be the last person to touch him. At least he was still wearing the embroidery thread bracelet that Devon made for him. He never took it off. That bracelet could be with him, could burn with him, for all of us.

I went through that first day in a blur, empty and numb and wondering what to do next. I emailed Elliot's boss and mine but asked that people not call. I didn't want to talk. I decided on a small family service on the weekend. That was all I could face. Elliot's mother, sister and children left the planning up to me. That made it easier, there was nothing to negotiate. I asked my mother to put together a lunch at my house afterwards. She would be good at that.

Devon wanted to go to school that day, Alex didn't. I let him stay home and watch TV. I started to throw out that medical crap that made it almost impossible to walk through my room. I lugged the forty-pound oxygen machine down the stairs—but lost my balance, hurt my shoulder and gouged a black scrape into the wall. Dragged it outside the front door. Shoved the shower chair out there. And the walker. And that godawful commode he used only once, such an indignity. Called the agency to pick up all that stuff, now. I wanted it gone. Tore through his drawers grabbing pills, vials, syringes. Hurled them into in a white garbage bag. The morphine "emergency kit" I never used, the Haldol, the OxyContin, the amphetamines, all that shit. Started moving faster and faster, like a wild woman, raging through the medicine cabinet, his nightstand, his knapsack, filling up the bag, bigger and bigger, until it was fatter than Santa's sack. I couldn't throw it in the trash because somebody might grab it and get high. I couldn't flush it down the drain because it would poison the water. I could sell it on the street to pay for a college education. But I called a friend married to a doctor to haul it all away.

Maybe Alex should have gone to school so he couldn't see me in such a frenzy.

At night I couldn't sleep. I obsessively tried to figure out if Elliot was suffering at the end. He seemed so distraught, confused, restless. His whimpering echoed in my ear. I cursed that godawful hospice, wished I'd found a better one. I tried to forgive myself. For the first time in my life I took Tylenol PM to knock myself out.

"Oh, Leslie, don't be haunted by this," the oncologist's nurse wrote back when I emailed her what happened. "You gave him the best care, love and attention that you could. And it is enough. He knew."

I tried to believe that doing my best was good enough.

I was alone when the man from the funeral home knocked at the door. He was carrying a translucent white shopping bag. It held a brass box. I carried it up the stairs in one hand. It—he—was heavy. But so much

194

easier than the last time we went up the stairs, when I lifted each impossibly leaden foot onto one step after another, and then had to call 9-1-1.

I didn't know where to put him. The closet seemed disrespectful. The bookshelf was too public. I settled on his bottom dresser drawer with his favorite sweatshirts, the ones from Ithaca and NYU and Michigan, the ones his children gave him when they went off to college. He loved them so much. It seemed weirdly informal, but that's where I thought he would be most at home.

I kissed my fingers and touched them to the dresser drawer, even though it felt silly.

I sat down to write a speech for his service and found that it gave me some peace. It felt good to spend time with him that way. It felt good to cry as I typed.

One morning, my friend Mary Jo came to our door with three bags of groceries from Whole Foods. Soups, salads, bread, fruit. She whirled around my kitchen, putting things away, finding a vase for flowers, setting them on the dining room table. She smiled, hugged me and left. Somehow some people know how to help.

I went to see Lissa, the counselor.

"How are you doing?" she asked.

"I'm here and I'm showered," I said. "That's enough."

There was a snowstorm right before the Saturday morning service, but our friends and family made it. Just two dozen people, like our wedding, but some of the friends had changed.

I cried through my speech. Our friends told beautiful stories. They cried for him, and they cried for us. I never expected to be an object of pity.

I stayed on my side of the bed. Took more Tylenol PM.

It was Christmastime. The kids and I trimmed a tree, decorated sugar cookies with red sprinkles and M&Ms even though our hearts were nowhere in it. When we opened presents, I pictured Elliot watching from the far side of a glass window, pounding madly on the glass to break through. He looked desperate to join us.

Devon and Alex left for a holiday trip planned long ago with their dad. I had an empty house, with three days free, for the first time in forever. Friends invited me over, but I wanted to be alone. I spent the silent hours sorting through emails, arranging photos and making a binder of condolence notes, obituaries and mementos for Elliot's mother. She turned that white book into an obsession, memorizing every word and weeping over it every day.

I had time to do what I had longed to do for years. I read over all of Elliot's love letters—a decade full of them—and put them in order. I luxuriated in them like a hot bath. They had his voice.

There was one card that he bought from a store, maybe because it spoke of a future he couldn't bear to frame the words for himself.

"Everything will be okay in the end," it read. "If it's not okay, it's not the end."

"That sounds about right to me," he'd written inside. "Love, E."

AND THEN

I knew I was loved. That gave me a backbone. I had children. They gave me a purpose.

And so I managed. I took a month off of work, took long walks and dealt with the endless paperwork of tying up a life—will, bank accounts, insurance. I buried myself in the distractions of minutia in hopes that by the time I surfaced, my raw wounds would have scabbed over, at least a little. I assigned myself strange, unnecessary chores born of fear, like hiring a man to put locks on our windows.

I checked the mailbox constantly for condolence cards. There were usually quite a few, full of kind words and other people's recollections, tidbits I'd never heard. When I wrote such cards in the past I'd always thought them trifling, wholly inadequate to the task. Now that I was on the receiving end, I was hooked. They were warm touches of concern. One *Record* reader sent me wise advice and even made me laugh: "Take things one day at a time, focus on your kids and stay away from country music."

Elliot's last night haunted me. I ordered his medical records from the hospice and showed them to a psychiatrist friend to see if they treated him right.

"He had such a bad cancer," I cried. "He deserved a good death."

"Why don't you think he had a good death?" the man asked gently. "He had perhaps some hours when he might have been medicated a little more optimally, but he was probably not aware. A merciful confusion sets in."

A bad death, he said, was dying alone in a hospital after languishing for months with nobody left who cares enough to visit.

"Elliot embraced his life fully," he went on. "I saw you two playing tennis not long ago. And he was with his family in the end."

That made me feel better. I had to cling to the hope that bit by bit, the passage of time would give me more perspective.

I began to say yes to every invitation. I even went to Elliot's book club. The men were meeting at our favorite cheap Thai restaurant. They had read Philip Roth's *Indignation*. It had been Elliot's suggestion. He would have loved it. It traced a young man, who, like him, was a straight-A student fleeing fiercely protective parents by going to a Midwestern college, desperate to find love and sex and romance. I felt proud, and glad, and grateful that we found that in each other.

"You do what you have to do to," Roth wrote.

And I did what I had to do. It was that simple.

Sometimes sorrow came down like an anvil. One morning my son came to the breakfast table wearing one of Elliot's ties. My heart stopped. I had asked Alex, Aaron and Max if they wanted to pick out a few. I didn't expect to see Alex wearing them to school. It was nice, though, to have those ties back in our lives, hanging on a doorknob at the end of the day.

Out of habit I still tore recipes out of *The Times* that I wanted to make for him.

It was hard to go to the A & P. I cringed when I passed by all those things I bought in bulk when Elliot could eat nothing else—Pepperidge Farm raisin bread, Nestle strawberry milk, Cranberry Almond Crunch cereal.

One day the paper had a photo of the demolition of Shea Stadium. Elliot was gone, and so was the stadium where he had felt so much excitement, disappointment and wild optimism as a boy and as a father. All that was over.

Yet there were unexpected pleasures. Once, I Googled Elliot's name. An old *Record* colleague I'd never met, Robin, had written about him for a blog called *The Perfect Moment Project*.

"The memory of one afternoon came back sharp and clear," she wrote. "I was at my desk, Elliot at his, juggling phone calls and people stopping by. The phone rang again and it was Max, Elliot's young son. Elliot was a little impatient at first but then I could just feel his body relax as he sat back. Elliot had decided to shut out everything else right then and give Max his full attention. I could tell from hearing one side of the conversation that Max had lost his Velociraptor and was pretty upset. Elliot, who took this loss as seriously as Max, talked his son through looking in his room, checking the kitchen and then pulling up the couch cushions where he found the toy. Emergency over. Max was back to playing, Elliot back to work…As sad as I am that Elliot has died, I am also comforted by the memory of that afternoon, happy that I witnessed that pure moment when he decided to cut out the clutter and help his boy, took the time to be a good dad."

That story was so Elliot. It was heartening to find that there was still more to learn about his life, and that he meant so much to so many.

A month after his death we held a big memorial service at the Montclair Art Museum. Almost two hundred people showed up, despite the snow, a truly lovely snow, gentle and soft. Aaron described their trip to Italy, Max talked about Elliot's encouragement for his writing. Kate was too shy to speak in front of the crowd but asked Max to read what she wrote about their childhood ritual of packing the Roadmaster for trips out West and detours to find blueberry pie.

Devon recalled how Elliot used to kiss her goodbye on the top of her head. "He gave me the stepbrothers and stepsister and steppeople—though I don't know technically what to call them now—that I will need to get through his loss."

You could barely see Alex's face over the podium. He stood on tiptoes. "Elliot gave me my first baseball glove," Alex said. "He took me to my first baseball game. He taught me the value of humor and happiness."

I wished that Elliot could hear them say these things. I wished we could all just be together now, with him, and move on as family from here, feeling so close.

I wished I could find him waiting for me in our bed.

WHY A WIDOW NEEDS A PUPPY

When President Obama told his daughters on election night that "You have earned the new puppy that's coming with us to the White House," my first thought was of my kids. They were the ones who deserved a dog. They had begged for years, but I kept saying no, I'm sorry, I can't take on responsibility for another living creature while Elliot is sick.

I couldn't say no anymore.

I thought I got our puppy for Devon and Alex. It turned that out Sadie, a blond Cockapoo born the day after Obama's inauguration, was the best medicine in the world for me.

1. She gets me up and out every morning for a walk.

2. Her enthusiasm is infectious. "Look! A blade of GRASS!" she seems to say as she bounces around in pure wonder. "Look! A LEAF!"

3. Never in my life have I talked so much to my neighbors. She forces me to connect with new people when my inclination might be to withdraw.

4. She licks our faces, crawls into our laps, and gives us the simple pleasure of her warmth.

5. The house never feels empty.

6. She lives in the moment. When Sadie pricks up her ears to hear a bird sing or rests her chin on my foot while I read the paper, I can't help surrendering to the here and now.

7. She lures my children to play together. She gives me the chance to watch their joy. She lets a boy express affection without worrying about being judged.

8. Kate, Max and Aaron get a kick out of her. She is family glue.

9. She doesn't hold a grudge.

10. She drags me outside in every kind of weather, in every season, reminding me that nature is change, spring will come, and there is always a promise of renewal.

"Elliot would have loved Sadie," Alex said as we walked her in the woods one day.

"Yes, he would have," I replied. "And he would love that we have her now."

Sadie as a puppy, spring 2009.

JIMINY CRICKET
Summer 2009

One day when the puppy was about six months old she leapt onto on my bed. That was quite a feat— it's a high mattress—and I had to make a snap judgment about whether to let her stay. I could hear the vet's stern voice in my ear.

"Don't let a puppy do anything you don't want her to do later," she warned.

I was probably supposed to nip this in the bud. I could picture Elliot's eyes rolling with dismay, especially when Sadie's wiggly butt settled on his pillow.

But I had come to like her grassy Milk Bone smell and the carefree way she flopped down wherever she felt like it. Who knew if there would ever be a man in my life who might object and so what if he did? I was tired of subjugating my desires to a husband's or a child's. This new stage of life seemed to be a rare time when I had leeway to indulge myself. If I had to put up with the hardships of being a widow at forty-eight, I should at least get to savor its small freedoms too. And so some nights I crawled into bed so exhausted I didn't bother to take off my work clothes. I made a whole meal out of corn on the cob. I relished eating dinner early with the kids instead of waiting, stomach gurgling, for Elliot's 7:40 train.

I tried to extend this sense of liberation to the bigger issues too. There were moments when I felt a kind of wonder that for the first time in a very long while I felt no pressure to meet a man or make one happy. Since high school it seemed I was always trying to find a boyfriend or keep him interested. I tried to please my first husband and succeeded in pleasing my second. So, by my count, for more than thirty years I worried, to one degree or another, about what a man wanted. Now, for better or worse, I could focus on pleasing only me.

And so, as I watched Sadie explore the yellow sheets on Elliot's side of the mattress—a place I have never ventured since he died—it surprised me to realize that I had even envisioned a far-off future with another man who might have an opinion about the rules for the dog. When I try to wrap my mind around that vision it escapes like a firefly. I still wear my wedding ring. I long to have my husband back, to sink into him at the end of the day. Yet as much as I miss Elliot, I do find it a relief to be released from his extreme needs for attention. I don't have the energy to take on the constraining burdens of anyone else's moods or schedules or children. So how can I even think, yet, about being part of a couple again? When I have pictured a first timid foray on an old-fashioned date, I have imagined Elliot watching from my shoulder like Jiminy Cricket, looking betrayed. "How can you do this?" he whispers. "What about me?"

That's my version of magical thinking. Joan Didion kept her late husband's shoes around because she figured he would need them when he came back to her. I have no delusions that Elliot will walk through our front door. My controlling vision is one of Elliot watching me with possessive eyes, accusing me of disloyalty if I ever find myself interested in anyone new. Then I lash out at myself for suppressing my own needs yet again to please him. Even when he is a ghost.

Once, at one of Alex's baseball games the spring before Elliot died, I bumped into a man I knew from *The Record* long ago. He was good-looking, my age, a reporter at *The Times* who had recently been divorced. We caught up for a few minutes and then I scurried back to my seat, afraid Elliot might think I was flirting, laying the groundwork for some future romance when he was gone. It rattled me to recognize a do-you-think-he-might-be-interested tingle. It seemed there was a tiny voice deep inside, much meeker than Jiminy Cricket's, suggesting it would be okay to find a man attractive someday.

The possibility of finding love again is something Elliot and I couldn't talk about when he was sick. I remember it coming up only once. I made it happen. I wanted to elicit his express permission that it would be okay, and understandable, if I ever ended up with someone else. Without such approval I would feel so guilty, so disloyal. It would feel like a betrayal.

"What am I going to do without you?" I asked on a drizzly Sunday afternoon as we walked to the movies. "How am I going to manage on my own?"

"You'll probably be remarried in six months," he teased, "and it will probably be to someone in my book group."

He dismissed the subject with a joking wave of his hand because it was too painful to entertain. It's impossible to imagine having a connection with any man like the one I had with Elliot. I don't even want that right now, but I would like to think that someday I would let myself be open to the idea. Who wants to wind up one of those crazy dog ladies who puts her poodle on dialysis and just marks time between bimonthly visits from grandchildren?

I'm a hypocrite, though; if I died before Elliot, it would kill me to picture him touching another woman. (There's that magical thinking again.) I would want him to put me and our marriage first forever. I would want him to be happy, but I would be jealous if he fell in love.

A friend once laid out the rules for her husband. "If I die you can marry a new wife," she said sportingly. "You just can't sleep with her."

Friends tell me the natural healing power of time will eventually sort all this out. Even Elliot's heartbroken mother has encouraged me to meet someone new. Six months after he died, I was on my way to a wedding—just to twist the knife deeper, it happened to be at our favorite getaway in the Berkshires, the Old Inn on the Green—when Helen called to wish me well.

"And you know," she added, "if some nice gentleman should ask you to dance, it wouldn't be a crime."

"Thanks, Helen, I'm really not in the mood yet," I said. "I'm not ready for any of that."

"You're young," she said. "I can't have another son, but you have to make a life for yourself."

That was very sweet to say, but please. She lost her husband twenty years ago and still wears his wedding ring.

So how long is long enough? When can you let go? A friend told me that when her mother died at a ripe age, the other women at the retirement community pounced on her father with their casseroles. He was one of the only men left and he still had a precious driver's license. There was a protocol among those in the brisket brigade: "Two weeks is too early, four weeks is too late."

Four weeks. Unfathomable.

Sometimes I look for clues in the newspaper. Here's a clip of an interview with Joyce Carol Oates, who got engaged within a year of losing her husband. That seems awfully fast. Here's a review of *Love Happens*, a Jennifer Aniston chick flick. The male lead is called "blocked" because he hasn't had a relationship since his wife died three years ago. So three years is seen as too long?

One thing is for sure, said a friend's mother, a reluctant expert after being widowed three times. "As long as you have your husband's ashes in your bedroom," she advised with a knowing nod, "you will not go on a date."

I don't want another man. I want Elliot back. He is not replaceable. Yet I don't want to wake up alone for the rest of my life either. Someday I will want to roll over and feel a man's warm strength. I will want to be spooned. Having tasted the joy of a rich marriage, I can't help wanting such happiness again. Not yet, but some day.

If I should ever marry again, I have a plan for my vows.

"Till death do us part," I'll say. "Me first."

At least, for now, I have a dog next to me where my husband used to be. I let her stay that day she jumped onto the bed, and she joins me any time she wants. I listen to her breathing, so peacefully. Curled on Elliot's pillow, she is adorable, unwitting proof of the enormous capacity of the human heart to keep making room for more.

GRATITUDE
Thanksgiving 2009

These manila folders full of recipes have so many memories. There is no organization to them, they're just thrown together in the order I found them or used them. I need some ideas about what to make for Thanksgiving, so I thumb through the yellowing, torn clips from newspapers and magazines and see evidence of so many dinners over the years. The Muscovy duck with cilantro, honey and pine nuts I made for a New Year's Eve dinner for Elliot, for just the two of us. We had it with champagne by the fire, sitting on the floor with candles on the coffee table, all dressed up, but not for long. Here's the recipe for sweet potato fries, "popular with the Pinsleys," reads my note to myself. Here's shrimp with lemon and capers. That one barely sounds familiar. When did I make that? So many things are lost, forgotten. That's why I write down what people say, or take videos, or keep seashells. I need them to remember. What vast swaths of experience have I lost because I didn't write them down?

We are having Thanksgiving on Saturday, two days after the real one, so Devon and Alex can be with their dad and the Pinsleys can be with their mom, and I can have them together when they are all free. I order butterflied leg of lamb from the Italian butcher. I just started going to Rosario's shop. He's one of the few men in my life now who says he wants to please me.

"It's nice the way our group is growing," Devon says while we get ready. She's right. There will be ten of us, thanks to Kate's boyfriend, Anthony; Aaron's fiancé, Sallie, and Sallie's sister, who is bringing her pint-sized mutt, Leroy Brown, a stray she found stranded on a golf course. Even without Elliot there will be more of us at the table.

I suggest they all come in the mid-late afternoon, maybe 4:00 or 5:00?

"We were thinking of pushing it earlier," Aaron calls to say. "How about 1:00? Then we can take a walk and hang out before dinner."

"Great," I say. "I was just going to be cooking and cleaning up."

"We'll help you," he says. It's so touching they want more time with us. I had said late afternoon so they wouldn't feel I was pressuring them – Aaron and Sallie are in from Chicago for only a few days and like to catch up with friends, and the last thing I want to be is an obligatory chore. And here they are the ones stretching out our day.

It is always a wonder to see how boisterous the Pinsleys are, even without their father here. We take the gentle mutt and our Sadie to the dog park, then come home and build a fire, and take videos of all the hubbub as everybody helps me bring up another table and chairs from the basement. I unfold a new gold tablecloth thinking maybe a change would be good but Elliot's mother wants the crimson one that I have always brought out for holidays. It's the one my mother used when I was little and it's showing battle scars like the rest of us. Who knew Elliot's mother would be as sentimental about it as I am? A year ago, when she needed to keep her hands busy while her son's body was falling apart, she spent a day darning the tablecloth with tiny black stitches. Maybe she needed to see there was something she had the power to fix. She reminded me of Penelope in *The Odyssey*, who kept weaving to keep away suitors until her husband came back. As if, by bending over that deep red fabric, Helen could keep away the worst kind of loss.

Aaron and Anthony have brought good wine. They are grownups now. They know to bring something to a dinner party. Aaron grills the lamb. He likes to be the man of the house. He does a beautiful job. It is charred on the outside but perfectly pink and juicy on the inside. It smells of garlic and rosemary and smoke. There are beets with goat cheese, and green beans roasted with radicchio, and saffron rice. We talk about when Max will graduate from college in May and what to do in Chicago when we fly out for Aaron and Sallie's wedding. Everyone interrupts each other but nobody seems to mind. I go upstairs for a minute and I hear them, laughing and unruly. And I realize I'm upstairs in my bedroom with my husband, his ashes are right here with me in the dresser drawer. I pretend he is with me for real. We are a couple, and we are listening to our family having a good time, and we are so proud of what we have built. I try to believe this is a sane thing to do.

Later, I am in bed, and I am tired, and I want to taste again how all this began. I open my box of Elliot's letters and pull out the first ones from the days we started dating.

"I think you entered my dreams for the first time," he writes. "What I remember is the two of us, reading the Sunday *Times* together…I was sprawled out on the couch, my feet up on the coffee table, reading the arts and leisure section, and you were lying lengthwise, your head in my lap, reading the magazine. There was sunlight on your face and I was running my hand through your hair. That's it. I suppose I could have told you that I grabbed you and ripped your clothes off and we rolled onto the floor and made wild love in a frenzy of passion. An appealing thought, but it didn't happen that way. I've thought about that picture all weekend, and in some ways right now, the peacefulness makes it more appealing to me. I want to do simple things with you."

I love that vision, so tender and serene. And here is another one from before we married. This one makes me cry. It is so full of yearning for our future.

"This relationship we have, it's like a delicate living thing, something to be enjoyed and treasured and protected. I don't want to do anything to jeopardize what we have because I want you in my life. I can't imagine it without you. I don't want to. What I want is to make you happy…

"I want to learn all I can about you because that place where you are is the best place I've ever been. I want to see how we are together, how we can be, and how far we can go and just enjoy that, to play and have fun and make love and be in love …and for that Leslie, I will always be grateful."

Grateful, I think. And I am grateful too. I had him, and I am trying to trust that I will find a way to feel him with me still as the years wander on. We could have gone a lifetime without finding such a marriage. We were lucky. I know I am even now.

"You have to make a new life for yourself," his mother tells me again on the phone. I understand what she means. But I have a life, a good life. I have our family, I have friends, I have a satisfying job. And that is enough, for now.

"If we are to live ourselves," Didion wrote, "there comes a time when we must relinquish our dead."

That time will come, I suppose, and maybe I will be thankful for that too.

But there is no rush. I am still pulled backward into memory, and that is something to cherish.

EVEN NOW
December 2009

In Devon's tenth grade art class, she was assigned to construct each member of our family in an abstract shape using white foam board. It touches me deeply that she included Elliot. It has been exactly one year since he died, and she still sees him as part of our home. Her three-dimensional design shows me and Elliot together as a parallelogram. Each of us is a triangular prism. Mine points up, supporting his. His points down and has a ghost's hollow core, but we fit together perfectly. We hold up a rod with a spikey flower on top. That is Devon, and she is linked to a large circle; she says that ring represents Alex, Kate, Max and Aaron, forged together through hardship.

I love that she sees us all together this way, and that she sees me and Elliot in such a balanced embrace, even now. I can learn from her vision. I am trying to find ways to feel him with me. And I do, sometimes. At night when I'm trying to fall asleep, I pretend his hand is on my hip.

This morning I went to a Zumba class at the Y with my new friend Laurie. We sashayed and swung our hips to the hot beat of salsa music in the basketball court. One of Elliot's best friends, Larry, happened to pass by the window; I could picture the two of them standing there, laughing as they kibbitized in the hallway on a break from their treadmills. They both had white towels around their necks to mop their sweat as they watched us kick and shimmy.

"Can you dance like that for me at home?" Elliot would ask later. "I want a private performance."

He looks sexy and mischievous in my daydream. So different from how I pictured him soon after he died, trapped behind a glass wall, pounding to break through.

And I realize, with happiness, I have seen a contented image of Elliot more often lately.

Kate comes over one night with her boyfriend and Max. I had asked earlier in the week if she wanted to get together Tuesday, the anniversary of her father's death, though I didn't say those words. She said thanks, no, but she felt like making a brisket on Friday for Hannukah. Although we'd never celebrated the holiday before, it sounds like fun. So she braises the meat in her oven and brings it to my house. I put out the new gold tablecloth, saving our ancient maroon one for Christmas. Alex lights a menorah and mumbles "baruch atai adonai…" with Max the way Elliot had taught them. This feels like the start of a yearly ritual, proof we can start new traditions even as we remain loyal to the familiar ones of our past.

Kate's brisket is the best I've ever had, tender and savory. She puts onions and sage in the applesauce for her latkes. It makes me ache. Elliot would be so proud of his daughter. Of this dinner. If only he could be here.

And then I decide I can see this differently. I can choose to be proud on his behalf. I can make myself envision him here with us. He would be beaming, and asking for seconds, maybe thirds.

"Katie-Pie," he'd say. "This is magnificent. Better than my grandmother's."

Sometimes happiness is a choice.

I am getting better at feeling this way.

I think back to the summer. To everyone's amazement my father was diagnosed with pancreatic cancer, just seven months after Elliot's death from the very same disease. I took Alex out to visit him in Sag Harbor for a few days. I made my dad melon ginger soup, soothing and light. He watched *The Four Feathers* with Alex to instill in him its respect for manhood, loyalty and honor. When Alex and I played basketball in the pool, I could feel my father feasting his eyes on us.

We knew my dad was very sick but didn't realize how soon the end would come. I had been promising all summer to take Alex to see the Mets in their new stadium, so we got tickets for a Friday night game. We hugged my father goodbye. I could feel his sharp shoulder blades under his navy blue robe. I turned away and then went back to him for another hug and kiss.

"One more for the road," I said. Then I hid in a bathroom to dry my eyes.

Alex and I drove to Citifield and got there at 5:00 p.m., two hours early. It began to pour. And pour. We ate pizza to kill time. Alex played a batting game, hit the target and dunked a guy on a platform into a vat of plastic balls. It kept pouring. Surely the game would be cancelled. An announcer called a rain delay. We waited some more. It was still pouring at 7:30. Then slowly it began to taper off. When men in uniforms trotted on to the field to peel back the tarp, the crowd erupted in a wild frenzy of cheers. We found our seats, wiped them off with sopping wet paper towels and sat down. In that instant the dark clouds parted, golden light sparkled off the greenest grass, and a giant Technicolor rainbow stretched clear across the heavens from one side of the stadium to the other. It was spectacular. Beyond breathtaking.

That's Elliot up there, I thought. He's congratulating us for our persistence. We stuck it out, it's game time, and he loves that we cared enough to stay despite the dismal odds. "That's my girl," he's saying up there.

I'll never forget that sky. It reminded me of that night a million years ago, after we soldiered through that first awful day at Sloan-Kettering and then drove out to Shea for Alex's tenth birthday. We just didn't give up then either.

Maybe this is what Elliot has taught me. To keep going. To feel his presence. Even after his death he helped me endure the loss of my father, just two days after that incredible rainbow. Because I had seen

Elliot suffer, I knew in my bones that my father's quick passage, only two weeks after his official diagnosis, was a gift. Because I knew how much Elliot would miss in our lives, I could appreciate how much it meant that my father got to see his daughters become mothers and his grandchildren become teenagers. My father had a rich adventure during his seventy-eight years on this earth, and I'm proud of the life he led.

"My tombstone should read 'He came to play,'" my dad had said. And that he did.

Who would ever have thought that someday I would have more experience as a widow than my mother? That she would turn to me for advice? That we would have this in common?

A few weeks after my father died, my mother, my sister's family and my kids went out on his beloved sailboat to bury him at sea. He would have liked the spot in front of the Shelter Island beach where my family had a house when I was little.

It was a drizzly afternoon. None of us felt like making speeches. My mother didn't want to do the tossing. She looked at my sister and me. I shook my head no. So Jessie took the bag of our father's ashes and stood up. A year older than me, she had always taken on the boat's harder jobs.

"Ready?" she asked. I nodded yes, and she threw the closed bag of dust. It was hard to fathom it was really our father. It landed with a splash and faded down below the gray-green water. My mother let out a sob. None of us said a word. In a nautical tradition, Jessie tossed in his white canvas sailing hat too. I watched the hat float on the choppy waves as the boat turned away.

Rain began to fall hard, and my heart felt like it was about to burst, so I went down the ladder into the cabin below. My kids followed me, and we sat close together on one of the cushioned benches. I had an arm around each one and kissed each one on the forehead. I breathed and simply felt them with me. Devon leaned her head against my shoulder. Alex started to cry.

In a little while we were calm again. The rain stopped and we came out of the cabin. The cool, salty air felt good. To my surprise, my sister whispered to me that during our little ceremony, she had almost cracked a joke. She reminded me of the days when we were kids and used to zip around this bay on a sunfish practicing lifesaving drills with our father just for fun. One of us would slip into the water at an unexpected moment. The first to notice would call out "man overboard" and whoever was at the helm would race to the rescue. Jessie said that when she threw our father's ashes, she was tempted to call out "man overboard" one last time. I couldn't help laughing. He would have laughed too.

It felt right to let go of my father that way. At his age, leaving was part of nature.

I still can't let go of my husband. And that feels right too. Elliot's ashes are still in his dresser drawer.

Next to the dresser, a set of wind chimes sat in their unopened package for more than a year. An exceedingly kind woman had given them to me. After she lost her seven-year-old daughter to cancer, someone had given her a set of chimes too, saying their music would let her hear Emily's voice in the wind.

I kept my chimes in their cardboard box because I was afraid their sound would kill me. I thought they would only taunt me with the absence of the husband I love so completely. But today, a glorious spring morning, I finally dared take the chimes out of their box and hung them in our yard in the sun. They sound beautiful in a gentle breeze. I found I like hearing Elliot in the air I breathe.

I am willing to believe, or pretend, or decide, that he is with me now, and he will be always.

LETTING GO
October 2010

Elliot used to say that big commercial movies finish with all the plot lines tied up in a neat bow, while independent films leave some loose ends dangling. So this story would be more of an indie, with good days and hard ones and questions still unanswered.

It's been almost two years since he died. I have dug in at work, where I now have a full-time job covering education, one of the hottest beats at the paper. At least for the moment, there seems to be an enormous appetite for news about contentious attempts to fire bad teachers, fix rotten test scores and turn around chronically failing schools. This stuff matters to me, and it gives me a kick that at press conferences, New Jersey's colorful Governor Christie calls on me by name.

My daughter, Devon, just got her driver's license. My son, Alex, only a baby when Elliot and I got together, is fourteen, with blond fuzz where a moustache wants to be. It seems like any minute they'll be heading off to college so I want to do things with them we'll never forget. The three of us went on a gorgeous vacation in Costa Rica, where iguanas crawled by our toes at breakfast and monkeys played at the beach. We took surfing lessons and were shocked to find we could get up. It was impossible to keep my balance in the waves but simply trying made me feel young and light and free. It didn't hurt to fall.

We've had some proud milestones. Max graduated from college in May and headed to Los Angeles to find a job in screenwriting. Elliot would be thrilled to see his youngest, the shy and serious one, taking such a daring leap. Aaron married Sallie in a lovely wedding in Chicago. They say they want to name their first son after Elliot. How I would love to give a tiny gurgling Elliot a very first kiss.

My personal milestone was a bit less dramatic. One day about a month ago I let Sadie off her leash in the woods so she could sniff around unencumbered. Usually when I did that she stayed close. Not this time. When a shaggy sheepdog lumbered by, she trotted after him and refused to come when I called her. I had to chase her down, blushing that I had so little clout.

"You can't blame her," said the dog's master. "My Cookie must be her Prince Charming."

I laughed as I bent down to grab Sadie's collar. When I looked up I saw a handsome man with dark hair, an amused grin and relaxed way of walking. He seemed a few years younger than me.

In the Julia Roberts version, we would stop to talk, hit it off and stroll off into the sunset with our smitten puppies in the lead. But the stranger kept going his way and I went mine.

That's when I took off my wedding ring. If I wanted such encounters to have a chance of leading somewhere someday, it didn't make sense to advertise myself as off limits.

Elliot would have to understand. As a wise counselor once told me, "Even when you lose the person you feel most connected to, you don't lose your deeply human need to connect."

The thought that maybe it was time to put away my ring had struck me once a few months before. My friend Lynn had invited me for a summer weekend at her family's country house in Connecticut, a gorgeous rustic cabin on a pond. We took a fifteen-mile bike ride with her parents, who were in their late seventies, still working and in fabulous shape. For thirty years I had admired their casual good looks and dedication to their careers in science and teaching. As we pedaled up the hills I marveled at their drive, especially when I noticed the scar on Lynn's father's back where he'd had major surgery the year before. Yet for all of their energy, and for all of Lynn's mother's beauty, their skin was more lined and their teeth seemed more fragile. Even this indefatigable couple was showing signs of wear. It dawned on me I would be lucky to be in such great shape at their age—and that was only about twenty-five years away. Not really much time at all. If I ever wanted to be part of a couple again, the window of possibility for meeting someone suddenly seemed small. Life is shorter than we think. Maybe I should wrench myself out of the past, sooner rather than later, or I'd be acting like one of those Indian women throwing herself on her husband's funeral pyre.

Surely Elliot wouldn't want that.

To my sentimental satisfaction, my finger is still indented where my ring used to be. Its shadow lingers as proof that he will always have his due influence.

"I hope I find somebody who loves me the way Elliot loved you," my daughter declared out of the blue as we were doing errands one day. "He couldn't have been more devoted."

My heart swelled. We taught our children what real married love can mean. I can't think of a better legacy.

Devon said I deserved to be happy with a man again and told me her daydream: This book would be made into a movie, and George Clooney would play Elliot.

"George will meet you on the set and fall in love," she said. "Then you can marry Elliot, in George's body, all over again."

On our last big family vacation with Elliot, he got a T-shirt from the lodge where we stayed in the Adirondacks. The shirt is maroon, and under the Hedges logo there's a hand-drawn picture of two people in a canoe on a lake surrounded by pine trees. The moon shines overhead. It's an image of utter tranquility.

"That's where I want to be right now," Elliot used to say as he pointed to the peaceful scene on his chest.

And so that's where he is.

Last weekend I took our kids back to the Hedges. It was perfect October weather. The leaves were glorious in the sun, all burnt orange and crimson and gold. I brought the brass box with Elliot's ashes in his black L. L. Bean knapsack. In a private moment I couldn't help unzipping the pockets. Yes, there were his computer screen wipes, umbrella and Trojans, as always. I smiled.

After breakfast Sunday the six of us headed out in canoes and made our way across Blue Mountain Lake towards a tiny island, really just an outcropping of rocks with a few evergreens.

"This is a beautiful spot," was all I could say. As we drifted silently in our canoes I held the brass box at an angle over the side and let the grey ashes fall bit by bit into the clear water. They were darker than my dad's, who knows why, and they swirled in a cloud under the ripples. In time the current pulled us away. We stayed quiet for a while, and then I wiped my eyes and took my paddle and began to head back to shore. The kids did the same. The wind picked up and blew against us. It became a challenge to move forward but we made it back to land eventually, one after another.

"That was a good idea," Kate said simply as we hoisted our canoes onto the dock. I think so. I like to imagine Elliot near the hiking he loved so much, someplace we all had fun together, with good food, wine, campfires, a porch with rocking chairs for reading and a magnificent view. There's something eternal about looking at the mountains.

It was hard to drive away. But sometimes you have to force yourself into the future.

EPILOGUE
2012

Every morning when I wake up I lie in bed for a while, looking through my window at the sunrise over Manhattan. For years there was a gap where the World Trade Center used to be, but recently an elegant new tower went up to fill that space. It's almost finished and taller than its neighbors.

Of course this tower can never replace what was lost. It reminds me, though, that I am certainly not alone in trying to rebuild a life, and new possibilities can come in time, if we let them.

ACKNOWLEDGMENTS

Here's a huge thanks to the army of great women who helped me through the past several years and made this book happen. They have fed, taught, encouraged and inspired me with unstinting generosity.

My good friend and writer Pamela Redmond Satran was the first to make me think I might be able to pull off something longer than a newspaper series. This project was a hazy glimmer of an idea until she took me out to lunch one day and said, "Let's talk about your book." Just hearing those words made it sound possible.

Then Pam brought me to a party where I met the indefatigable Laurie Lico Albanese. Laurie, a novelist, mentioned she taught a college course on writing memoir, and she agreed on the spot to teach me too. And so for many months I spent Wednesday nights in Laurie's attic with two other women learning how to spin small moments into personal narratives. Those hours of empathy, sidesplitting laughter and occasional tears sustained me through that first uncertain year as a widow. When the future looked so blank, Laurie's warmth, humor and conviction that I could finish a manuscript gave me a sense of purpose. Even more, we became close friends.

My loyal friends from high school and college took the baton. When I was dithering about whether and how to look for an agent, they urged me on. Profound thanks to Lisa Noveck Buseck, Susan Briggs, Claudia Meininger Gold, Linda Schupack, Alexandra Shelley and Nancy Youman. Maggie Jackson and Lynn Novick went way beyond the call—more on them later.

My savvy, tenacious and wonderfully caring agent, Judith Ehrlich, willed this book into print. Her faith in this project and dedication to details were deeply moving. Sophia Seidner, her colleague at Judith Ehrlich Literary Management, added her keen intuition and skills. Thanks also to my publisher, Tracy Ertl, who was excited by the manuscript from her first reading and welcomed me into the TitleTown fold.

At *The Record*, my compassionate editors Susan DeSantis and Deirdre Sykes gave me the flexibility my family needed. My fellow reporters Patricia Alex, Mary Jo Layton and Lindy Washburn made coming to work fun, thanks to their talent, irreverence and hilarious lunchtime updates.

My book group has been a rock for more than a decade. Somehow I brought more than my share of drama to our monthly meetings. Here's a toast to Jean-Marie Menk, Cindy Carlson, Marcia George, Sheri Karvelas, Nancy Kopilnick, Sue McKeown, Frazer O'Neill, Tracy Parsons and Nancy Tortoriello.

I hope these women never find themselves in circumstances where they need my support the way that I needed theirs. But if they do, I hope I will be there for them the way they were always there for me.

It's time to add a few men to the mix. Several couples were stalwarts and figured out ways to help us before we even knew what we needed. My deepest appreciation to Lynn Novick and Robert Smith; Pam and Dick Satran; Maggie Jackson and John Hitchcock; Mary Ellen Schoonmaker and Mike Hoyt; and Celia Radek and Larry Engelstein.

Elliot's colleagues at *Bloomberg News* were incredibly sensitive to his needs, while his book group buddies cheered him on and distracted him with their ridiculous rescheduling rituals.

Special thanks to the fantastic friends of Devon and Alex, especially the families of Diana Lawson and Jack Ross, who gave my kids another set of warm, loving and endlessly entertaining homes when they needed a refuge. We are so lucky to have you.

Thanks as well—for an array of reasons—to Helen Pinsley, Anastasia Rubis, Sallie Scherer, Anthony Brinton, Janet Wicka, Milo

Geyelin and our neighbors at the top of our hill.

On the medical front, we were very fortunate to get help from the expert, extremely hard-working staff at Memorial Sloan-Kettering Cancer Center, especially Dr. David Kelsen and his nurse, Jenny Jenkins.

My mother, Jackie Brody; sister, Jessica Nagy; and her family of Lee, Summer and Ernie have stuck by me with care and generosity, helped me raise my kids, and always made sure they wore sunscreen.

There are not enough words to express my gratitude to my father, Gene Brody, whose confidence in me meant so much.

Needless to say, I wish Elliot could be here and could read what amounts to a last love letter. I wish he could see how well our kids are doing and what they've become. I wish he could meet his first grandchild, a gorgeous baby girl named Juniper.

I couldn't be more proud of them.

The biggest thanks of all go to Alex, Devon, Max, Kate and Aaron.

I hope this book will help them remember.

READING GROUP GUIDE

In "The Last Kiss," Leslie Brody shows how she and her husband, Elliot, made the most of their vanishing time together while he was fighting pancreatic cancer. The book shows the life-affirming power of a passionate marriage, the importance of loyal friends and the resilience of children. A newspaper reporter for more than twenty years, Leslie says this is the most important story she has ever told.

1. If you learned you had two years left to live, how would you change your life right now? If you learned your husband or wife had two years left, how do you imagine your reaction might be different?

2. At what point does Leslie seem most conflicted? How does she face the unanswerable elements of her situation?

3. Leslie bristles at insensitive comments people make about Elliot's illness. What rude things have people said to you in times of crisis? What would have been more helpful? How did you respond?

4. Has a tragedy changed your religious views in some way? How?

5. When Leslie tells her children that Elliot used medical marijuana before it was legal, she says that sometimes you have to break the rules to do the right thing. Have you ever broken a law, or under what circumstances would you do so?

6. After an embarrassing quarrel in the chemo unit with Elliot, Leslie says "maybe a marriage is like muscle that you have to strain and flex and stretch to strengthen." How does this image apply to your own life?

7. For better or worse, in sickness or health. Have you wondered how far you would go to uphold these vows? Would you follow the advice that Leslie embraced, "Don't be afraid to grow closer?"

8. What role does food play in the evolution of Leslie's stepfamily? How do you see food—as either a source of togetherness or tension—in your family's life?

9. Leslie doesn't shield her children from the sad physical realities of their stepfather's deterioration. How do you see her decision?

10. The book shares Elliot's intimate emails and letters. Is that an invasion of his privacy? What are the pros and cons to you as a reader?

11. Leslie and Elliot never really talk directly about death or how she would take care of their family after he dies. How do you feel about that choice?

12. At the end of the book, Leslie feels deeply torn about when—or even whether—to start dating again. What would you do, and how long would you wait? How long would you want your partner to wait?

13. What is the symbolism of the peach that Leslie sketches and then eats with Elliot? "We live for moments like this," she says. What is a moment in your life that stands out this way?

14. Besides the written and spoken word, how do Leslie and Elliot show their love for each other? Are some ways of expressing love more meaningful to you than other ways?

15. What might you do for a partner or lover to help make the final days—or the last kiss—the best possible?